WfT

West's Federal Taxation

Tax Return Preparation with TurboTax®

for WINDOWS

Personal/1040, Version 97.01

Contains 1997 Tax Forms

Jerrold J. Stern
Indiana University

Intuit®
San Diego, California

WEST/SOUTH-WESTERN College Publishing

An International Thomson Publishing Company

Publishing Team Director: Rick Lindgren
Sponsoring Editor: Alex von Rosenberg
Developmental Editor: Esther Craig
Production Editor: Barbara Fuller Jacobsen
Marketing Manager: Maureen Riopelle

ISBN 0-538-88905-5 (packaged manual and CD-ROM)
ISBN 0-324-00212-2 (manual only)

1 2 3 4 5 6 7 8 9 MZ 6 5 4 3 2 1 0 9 8

Printed in the United States of America
I(T)P®
International Thomson Publishing
WEST/South-Western College Publishing is an ITP Company.
The ITP trademark is used under license.

PREFACE

West's Federal Taxation Tax Return Preparation with TurboTax manual is designed to support the use of TurboTax in the classroom. TurboTax is a widely-used tax return preparation software package. Most tax professors are quick to point to the advantages of having students complete tax returns; some also point out the related problems. Two of these are: (1) time-consuming redundancy that occurs when students transfer data between tax forms, and (2) having an adequate supply of tax forms with related instructions. TurboTax offers solutions to both of these problems.

First, TurboTax can be very "tax form" orientated (depending upon the input method selected). The student has to examine the forms and related worksheets (displayed on screen) and complete each by entering data. An advantage with electronic tax return preparation is that the student does not have to do excessive computations or copy information from one form to another. With the graphical ability of Windows, each form displayed on the screen is virtually identical to official IRS forms. Second, several TurboTax worksheets are interactive, i.e. the worksheet leads the user through a complicated area of the tax law by asking relevant questions. Third, the student has on-line access to the major IRS forms and related instructions. The IRS instructions are accessed through the TurboTax HELP menu. TurboTax helps the student find the answer by entering the instructions at the location that is related to the current line or form. Thus, the student learns from the very beginning to identify tax problems, research the answer and report the results correctly on tax forms.

This version of TurboTax is limited to individual tax returns. Other versions of TurboTax, discussed briefly in Chapter 2, support the preparation of Partnership returns (Form 1065) and Corporation returns (Forms 1120 and 1120S). By using TurboTax to prepare individual tax returns, students can learn much about tax law, tax return preparation, and use of tax technology. TurboTax can be used by students either in a PC Lab environment or on their own individual PCs.

You can use TurboTax to prepare returns in either of two ways: (1) the EasyStep® Method or (2) the Forms Method. EasyStep is designed as a "guided tour" and is best for a student's first attempt at tax preparation. The Forms Method is faster, but requires greater knowledge of tax forms. The manual discusses the methods in detail in Chapters 3 and 4.

Each year, TurboTax enhances its software for users. New features for 1997 include:

1. **1997 Tax Act** - TurboTax includes all of the tax law changes made by the Taxpayer Relief Act of 1997. Users are given guidance to help them take advantage of every deduction.

2. **Improved Navigation** - An improved Search feature enables you to locate any part of your tax return with a mouse click.

3. **Customized Interview** - The EasyStep Method has been made faster and more efficient by automatically focusing questions on issues relevant to a user's specific tax situation. TurboTax accomplishes this by tailoring all questions based on answers to previous questions.

4. **Tax-Saving Tips for 1998** - Tax Report provides personalized tax tips to help plan to reduce the taxpayer's 1998 taxes.

The decade of the 1990's is an exciting time for the development and application of technology to tax practice. Several firms are developing career paths for tax accountants who specialize in tax technology. All tax students are expected to know how to use various types of technology before they begin their first day of professional employment. Electronic tax return preparation may be the very first assignment for a newly-hired accountant even if the accountant's responsibilities include a substantial amount of nontax work. Thus, learning to use TurboTax will help provide the entry-level skill set required.

Tax return preparation is not the only use of technology by tax advisers. The ability to use electronic tax research services on CD-ROM and the World Wide Web is equally important. Also, the use of E-mail to communicate with clients and other tax advisers is another expected use of technology. Another source of tax information includes online services (such as Lexis and RIA). Without question, all tax advisers need to be able to use technology effectively.

For more information about Intuit products, including TurboTax, Quicken, QuickBooks, ProSeries and other excellent products used by accountants and business professionals, there is a brief discussion at the beginning of Chapter 2, "Overview of TurboTax." For further details, see their sites on the World Wide Web at the following URLs:

http://www.turbotax.com
http://www.intuit.com

You must have your own browser software. If you do not have a browser, use the Microsoft Internet Explorer included in this package and take a look at the web. You must be familiar with the information available on the Internet. The volume of information on the Web is overwhelming; the amount of useful information is large. The problem you have to contend with is discerning the difference between that which is, and that which is not useful.

TURBOTAX IN THE CLASSROOM

The primary focus of most tax courses is to give the student an understanding of how the tax system works and the basics of tax law. The tax return preparation process is considered a secondary topic that may in fact be passed over by some professors. However, the first tax job of most students will be to prepare some type of tax return. In addition, an understanding of the various tax forms helps the student understand how different areas of tax law are related. Thus, tax return problems are frequently assigned to students.

In 1992, the Committee on Computer Applications of the American Taxation Association conducted a survey of tax accounting professors. The survey covered three areas:

1. Reasons for using computers in tax education
2. What software is used by tax accounting professors
3. What courses use computer technology

While some of the study's findings are dated, it nonetheless reports major reasons for using or not using computers in tax education that are relevant today. The primary reasons for using computers in tax education as reported by tax accounting professors are that they:

1. Prepare student for real-world situations.
2. Increase emphasis on tax planning

Others reasons for using computer technology are that it

3. Facilitates learning basic tax topics.
4. Keeps the tax course on the cutting edge of tax education.
5. Increases efficiency in teaching tax topics.

The primary reason that computers are not used in tax education is the lack of time available to cover necessary topics in the course. A second reason reported is the lack of software useful in teaching of tax topics.

TurboTax supports the use of computers in tax education in several ways. First, TurboTax follows the design of the paper tax forms. Thus, inputting tax data in TurboTax gives students the same learning experience as manually writing the data on a paper form. It is true that the software will automatically carry forward the total amounts to the correct line on Form 1040. As a result, students will not experience the clerical task of carrying forward totals as instructed on the forms. Some argue that, without this task, students will tend to not read the forms closely. However, students will be able to see how the forms are related to each other. This is one way the software adds value to the tax learning process.

The purpose of this manual is to relieve professors from having to spend classroom time instructing students how to use the software. Thus, the learning time required is added to the student's time spent outside of class. Of course, student time is limited and valuable. But, the more time students spend learning tax concepts, rules and computations, the better equipped they will be to face the many challenges of being a professional accountant.

In addition to tax preparation, TurboTax's "What-if" option is very useful as a tax planning aid. The user can compare the tax results under four alternatives using the **Tool Menu** option, **What-if**. TurboTax also supports the computation of the tax using estimated 1998 rates and tax law. The combination of a forms orientation and the "What-if" option make TurboTax very supportive of the primary reasons for using computers in tax education. Perhaps this is the reason the survey of tax professors found TurboTax to be the most used tax preparation software in tax accounting education.

An analysis of the users of computer technology in tax education indicates that the discriminating application between users and non-users is electronic tax research. Today's focus of tax technology is on the ability to use advance applications to eliminate the more procedural tasks. TurboTax aids both of these desired ends in two ways. TurboTax provides a user-friendly interactive interview, referred to as "EasyStep." This is a series of questions designed to guide the tax preparer through the return. As the student answers questions related to the taxpayer's transactions, TurboTax transfers the data to the appropriate tax form. The EasyStep method may be said to "take students by the hand and lead them through the tax return."

TurboTax's HELP function is context sensitive. Thus, when you move the cursor to a specific line and select HELP, TurboTax displays the help options for that specific line. The availability of detailed IRS instructions and TurboTax tax aids, displayed on the screen almost instantly, allows tax students the opportunity to examine on their own, less complex areas of tax law not covered in class due to time constraints. The Help function also provides the option of searching the Help topics using key words, similar to the method used by electronic tax research products, such as *Lexis* and RIA's *OnPoint.*
Thus, students have the opportunity to learn techniques useful in electronic tax research.

In summary, the use of TurboTax in a tax class has specific advantages over other tax preparation alternatives. The student will be able to view the tax forms on the screen and learn the organization of the various forms without the clerical burden of arithmetic and copying the same information several times as the data is moved from a detail supporting form to Form 1040. Users of the software have consistently indicated that it is easy to use and requires very little class time. This manual is written in a casual style that is intended to be easy to read. And for support in understanding the tax law, students have both TurboTax tax aids and online IRS instructions available at the touch of a key. Lastly, even though this version may not be used by paid preparers, the new tax professional is exposed to tax return preparation as it is done in the "real world." The best way to understand the advantages and disadvantages of using tax return preparation software is to use it. Using TurboTax helps young tax advisors prepare for the professional world they are about to enter. This manual provides 30 tax problems to give you practice in using TurboTax. We all know that "practice makes perfect."

TABLE OF CONTENTS

CHAPTER 1

INTRODUCTION

The 1990s is a decade of automation in professional practice by tax advisors. Technology is growing in importance in every aspect of business including the professional practice of tax advisors. In fact, the tax advisor of today cannot practice without the use of tax technology. The term "tax technology" refers to the use of computer and related technology in tax practice. Thus, "tax technology" can be defined as the use of computers, software, printers, communication hardware and storage devices in tax practice.

The core of tax technology is computerized tax return preparation and tax research (via CD-ROM, the World Wide Web or an on-line service). In the professional world, computers have been used to reduce the amount of clerical activities required to complete a tax return. The time saved has allowed tax advisors to spend more time analyzing the increasingly complicated tax laws that face today's taxpayers.

In addition to tax preparation and tax research, other uses of tax technology are:

- the use of specialized tax planning software referred to as Tax Decision Support Software,
- the use of electronic spreadsheets for tax planning,
- the use of communication hardware and software for electronic filing,
- the use of office automation tools for word processing and electronic mail, and
- the use of the Internet to access new and innovative sources of tax information.

The purpose of this manual is to support your use of TurboTax in preparing tax returns. The software that is included with this manual is "TurboTax for Windows, 1997 Version" by Intuit. The software is NOT a student version. In fact you will be able to prepare your personal tax return with the software. This version of TurboTax provides you with the all the forms and schedules that you are likely to need.

This manual is designed to be used by students who aspire to be professional accountants, who have recently begun to learn tax law and who are not experts in using personal computers. It is intended to be a user-friendly manual.

Before you begin using TurboTax, you should learn about the big picture of tax return preparation. Accordingly, in the sections below, you will read about the tax return preparation process and take a brief look at tax return preparation software in general. If you cannot wait to begin using TurboTax, go directly to Chapter 2. (Do not pass GO, and you certainly will not collect $200.) You can come back to Chapter 1 later.

TAX RETURN PREPARATION PROCESS

Prior to filing a tax return, tax information must be gathered, summarized according to tax accounts and entered on the appropriate tax form. Regardless of whether a tax return is prepared manually or with the aid of a computer, the steps followed are similar. The general steps in filing a tax return are as follows:

- Gather and summarize tax data.
- Research tax return preparation questions.
- Enter tax data on the appropriate return and document the source of the data used.
- Review the tax return.
- File the tax return.

Gathering and Summarizing Tax Data

Typically, the most painful part of preparing an individual tax return is reviewing past transactions to gather the necessary information. The effort required depends upon the economic circumstances of the taxpayer involved and the method the taxpayer used to store transaction information and documentation (i.e., receipts, canceled checks, statements, etc.)

With business returns, the information normally is contained in a general ledger accounting software package. Typically the information will be organized by account numbers and a trial balance will be available. If the information has been audited, the amounts are assumed to be "correct" for tax preparation purposes. If the information is unaudited, the information should be reviewed to identify possible errors. The review will normally require the detailed accounts be reviewed and some source documents examined to ensure the data are correct. Even though the purpose of the data review is to prepare a tax return, the professional standards of the accounting profession (as set forth in Statement of Responsibilities in Tax Practice No. 3) requires that the tax return preparer "... not ignore the implications of information furnished and should make reasonable inquiries if the information appears to be incorrect, incomplete or inconsistent either on its face or on the basis of other facts ..."

If the information has been audited, an audited trial balance is the source of tax data. The job of a tax return preparer is to regroup the accounts to reflect the information needed for the tax return. Many software packages used in the audit process provide an optional account grouping that will automatically reorganize the accounts in a format suitable for tax reporting. This tax grouping must be coded at the time that the various accounts are set up in the auditing software. If audit software has not been used in the audit, the tax return preparer will have to regroup the accounts with a worksheet -- manual or electronic.

If the information has not been recorded or summarized, the tax return preparer will have to develop a chart of accounts that corresponds to the lines on the tax return, and enter the details of each transaction into the appropriate account. Many tax return preparers refer to this situation as the "shoe box" approach, so called because many taxpayers choose a shoe box to store their receipts, checks, and other documentation of yearly transactions. Use of a simple electronic worksheet, general ledger software, or trial balance software will lessen the pain and shorten the time required to prepare a return.

With the advent of the personal computer, many individuals are using family financial management software to record cash receipts and disbursements in the same manner as a general ledger accounting software package. Tax return preparation software supports the direct interface of most financial management/accounting software. If supported, the financial data can be summarized with the accounting software and directly imported to the tax return preparation software. TurboTax supports direct interface with *Quicken®* and *QuickBooks®* (using the **TaxLink** command) and other financial programs (using txf). Other financial management programs that use "Tax Exchange Format" (TXF) files are supported with the general interface command, **Import**, discussed in Chapter 4. In late 1993, Intuit, the creator of *Quicken®* purchased ChipSoft, Inc., the creator of TurboTax. Thus, there is a high level of integration between the two software programs. However, the general acceptability of TXF files means that tax preparation software like TurboTax will interface with a wide variety of general ledger/accounting software packages.

The normal order used in gathering information follows the organization of the tax return. First the taxpayer's name, address, and identifying numbers are recorded. Next the income items are gathered and entered on the return -- electronically or manually. Then the deductions are identified. If available, the previous year's tax return should be reviewed in order to identify recurring transactions. If tax preparation software is used, the software carries over continuing items (such as names, income sources, depreciation schedules, etc.) to the next year. With TurboTax, the **Transfer** command is used to copy relevant information from the prior year tax return to the current year tax return.

The importance of a continuing file of prior year's tax returns cannot be overstated. Information as to the previous year's income from various types of property can lead to discovery of gains or losses from the sale of such property. Similarly, sources of income from the previous year, can be expected to continue into the current year. Thus, comparison of current year's information with the previous year's is crucial to the tax return preparation process.

Data gathering is the first and frequently the most time consuming step. After the data have been gathered, the taxability of the transactions must be determined. Often, tax return preparers will have to research various sources of tax law to determine how to report the transaction on the tax return.

Researching Tax Return Preparation Questions

In recent years the tax laws have become so complex that tax return preparers are reluctant to express opinions on the tax status of a transaction without referring to tax reference materials. The source of the tax reference depends upon the tax return processing method selected. If tax preparation software is used, the software may provide an online tax reference indexed to the specific line on the tax form. The tax reference materials used by TurboTax are the TurboTax tax aids, "plain-English explanations of what to enter for the selected tax form line," and the "official" IRS instructions to forms. Professional versions of some tax preparation software, like Intuit's ProSeries, interface directly with CD-ROM tax research materials such CCH's *ACCESS*, RIA's *OnPoint* or online services such as CCH's *Access Online*. Of course, other online electronic services such as WestLaw or Lexis, as well as paper tax research materials are also available.

The goal in researching return preparation questions is to determine the correct tax result of a **completed** transaction and the correct location on the tax return to report that transaction. Typically, a formal research report is not prepared, but a complete list of references, and a statement of research conclusion is required. In most cases, reference to a secondary source, such as a publishing company's editorial comments, is acceptable. If the amount of tax at risk is "large," a formal tax research report, citing **primary sources** of tax law (e.g., Internal Revenue Code, Treasury Regulations, court cases, IRS rulings, etc.) should be prepared and kept on file in case there is an IRS audit. In some cases, your research will not result in an answer about which you have 100 percent confidence. This occurs when the correct answer must be deduced from related court cases, rulings, or regulations. In these situations, the research report should clearly set forth the logic that links the taxpayer's facts with primary sources of tax law and the conclusion reached by the researcher.

Techniques for documenting the results of tax research vary among firms. The overriding objective is for the tax researcher to provide a trail from the specific item in question to the tax research materials used. With electronic tax return preparation, electronic notes can be added to document the research performed and the results of that research. Of course, memos to the taxpayer client file can also be created.

Documentation of tax return data

The preparer's declaration on tax returns states that the information contained therein is true, correct, and complete to the best of the preparer's knowledge and belief, "based on all information of which the preparer has any knowledge." The statement is understood to relate to all information provided by the client or third parties. Accordingly, the tax return preparer may be asked to produce documentation of the source of information used in return preparation. At the present time, the IRS expects documentation in paper form. Examples include copies of canceled checks, copies of Form 1099, copies of trial balances, copies of invoices for large expenditures, lists of records kept by taxpayer and their location, and copies of financial statements. If the return is prepared with tax preparation software, the tax return preparer will need to maintain a paper file with copies of all information provided in addition to the electronic file generated by the tax preparation software. If data are provided to the preparer in electronic form, a trial balance from a general ledger file for example, a copy of the electronic files should be kept by the preparer. While not tested in the courts, the acceptability of electronic files as evidence is so similar to that of microfilm, which is fully accepted by the Federal Rules of Evidence, that tax return preparers are able to record information electronically and do away with paper storage. However at the current time, tax return preparation software will be used to create a paper tax return and paper supporting documents will normally be stored in the same manner as if the returns were prepared manually.

One of the developing problems of the last half of the 1990's is the increasing use of Electronic Data Interchange (EDI) by most large companies and many smaller companies. With EDI, there is no paper trail. Tax auditors are uncomfortable in such an environment and they pass on their feelings to the tax preparer. An example is Revenue Procedure 91-59, 1991-2 CB 841 in which the IRS requires "that all machine-sensitive records generated by a taxpayer's ADP system are retained so long as they may be or may become material in the administration of any internal revenue law." In this age of fast changing technology, does this mean that the taxpayer must keep old operating systems available that can read the files created four or more years ago? Imagine trying to read a 5.25 floppy disk formatted with DOS 2.1. Many PCs today simply cannot do it. Add the problems of the firm that has changed from DOS to UNIX or some other operating system and the problems multiply. When everyone created a paper trail, the format of the data was not a problem. With an EDI system in place, operating system and format problems float to the surface.

Welcome to the Information Age!

Reviewing the Return

The normal steps in the preparation of a tax return include a review of the return by someone other than the preparer. In the case of a preparer who works alone, that review is normally done on another day so that the data and return may be given a fresh look. In either case, the goal is to detect any errors or omissions. The use of tax return preparation software makes it possible to create an all electronic tax file. All notes from the taxpayer and all tax data may be recorded electronically, eliminating the need for a paper file. However, if tax preparation software is used and no paper files are kept, the reviewer will have nothing to refer back to. At this time, paper files should still be kept. The IRS will accept an electronic record in support of a tax return if that is the way the initial transaction is recorded. Scanning of paper documents for storage purposes has not yet been considered by the IRS. Thus, while the availability of electronic filing does allow a paperless tax return, most tax preparers still maintain a paper record of the taxpayer interview and refer to that paper in the review process.

The tax profession has not fully addressed these complications. As noted, current practice is to require a paper record of the interview with the taxpayer. Also, as noted above, paper copies of all information provided should be kept. At this time, the full productivity gains available with electronic tax return preparation are not being realized. Most tax preparation software does provide an online internal check of the return. Generally, this checks for consistency in the data entered and for completeness of data entered. The TurboTax command for this procedure is named **Final Review**. Thus, currently, the review of a computer prepared return is being conducted similarly to the review of a manually prepared tax return.

Filing the tax return (Delivery to the IRS)

As we approach the year 2000, the IRS is working on its procedures to expand electronic filing. Starting in 1988, the IRS allowed selected preparers to file electronic tax returns if the return resulted in a tax refund. Currently, over 16 million tax returns are filed electronically. Procedures have been finalized to allow a tax due return to be filed electronically. One problem with electronic filing is that the advantage is primarily to the IRS. For refund due returns, the IRS promises a faster turnaround time, which has encouraged taxpayers to request electronic filing. However, for tax due returns, there is little advantage to the taxpayer. Currently, electronic filing must be followed by a paper copy of the return, which eliminates any cost savings to the preparer that could have been passed on to the taxpayer in the form of lower fees. Accordingly, while both possible and efficient, electronic filing has not yet gained the same level of acceptability among tax return preparers that it promises. At the December, 1994 meeting of the AICPA Tax Division, the director of electronic filing for the IRS predicted that by the year 2001, 63% of all returns will be filed electronically and electronic filing will be the "preferred method" of filing. However, the General Accounting Office (GAO) has been consistent and strong in its criticism of IRS efforts to automate the filing process. Recent reports in the business press state the IRS has not yet adopted a strategic plan that will culminate in a comprehensive strategy that will help the IRS achieve its goal of 80 million electronic filers by the year 2001. The GAO has noted that the IRS plan to use scanners to scan paper tax returns has not been successful. Currently, it is questionable whether the IRS scanning procedures will produce benefits greater than the related costs. The only form currently being scanned is Form 1040EZ.

The AICPA Tax Division's Tax Computer Applications Committee conducts occasional surveys of its members on the use of technology in tax practice. The 1993 survey reports that 13.7 percent of the respondents file returns electronically. Also, this survey reported that 19 percent of the respondents planned to file electronically in 1994. While the reason may be competitive pressures and not efficiency, it is clear that there is a trend to increased use of electronic filing. Accordingly, tax preparation software generally provides a module to support electronic filing. In fact, some authors report that electronic filing is "... the drummer to which all software packages must listen, if not march." Tax preparation software in the 1990's must support electronic filing; TurboTax does.

In summary, the primary impact of computerized preparation on filing the return (rather than its preparation) is the amount of time savings available in the copying and collating process. A paper return is printed, signed, and mailed to the IRS similarly to that done with manually prepared tax returns. Until electronic filing is made more attractive, filing the return prepared with a tax preparation software package will involve the same steps as a manually prepared return.

ELECTRONIC TAX RETURN PREPARATION

There are significant advantages to the use of computers in tax return preparation. These advantages are listed in an AICPA Tax Division's document, *Automation of the Tax Practice of the '90s*. While this document is currently under revision, its major points are still valid. The major advantages of automation listed are:

1. Perform work more quickly.
2. Produce higher quality work in the same amount of time.
3. Consider more alternatives in the same amount of time.
4. Produce a better looking work product.

Tax return preparation software operates in three basic modes:

1. In-house
2. Service center
3. Mixed in-house and service center

The 1993 AICPA Tax Division's Tax Computer Applications Committee annual survey reported that the respondents used in-house computerized tax preparation on more than 90 percent of the tax returns they prepared. In a 1992 article in *Journal of Taxation*, Nelson and Langer estimated that approximately 72 percent of returns filed by professional preparers were prepared with in-house computer processing. They also estimated that 11 percent were prepared using an outside service center. Manual return preparers filed 17 percent of the returns. The basic differences in these three modes of processing returns are briefly discussed below.

In-House Processing

The most common form of processing tax returns with computers is in-house processing. In-house processing refers to the use of software and hardware owned by the preparer. None of the tax data leaves the preparer's location. Typically the preparer will purchase professional tax preparation software from a software developer, such as Intuit Inc., the developers of ProSeries (Professional Version) and TurboTax (Personal Version). The entire tax return process, from input of data to printing of the final return is done in-house, i.e., on the preparer's premises. There are significant advantages, some of which are listed here:

- Source documents do not leave the premises, therefore confidentiality is maintained.
- Tax data can be entered directly in the computer without taking the time to transcribe the data.
- Turnaround time is fully under the control of the preparer.
- The cost structure is shifted from a variable cost to a fixed cost.

The advantages do not come without disadvantages. The major concern is that the preparer must identify the best preparation software for the firm and purchase that software on an annual basis. Tax return preparation software developers have been generally reliable (i.e., they have stayed in business.) However, there have been occasions when the developer has lost key personnel, resulting in future revisions containing errors. In such cases, the preparer may have to change software during a very busy time of the year. The time required to learn a new software product is costly. If the same software is used annually, the required training cost is minimized.

The cost of hardware for an in-house system is easily justified. In the early days of computer tax preparation, the cost of hardware was a constraint to in-house processing. However, the cost of computer processing has come down greatly. Today you can purchase one year old technology for under $2,000. Any tax return preparer can justify that expenditure. Thus, the cost of hardware is no longer a constraint.

Service Centers

A service center is a company that provides computer services to users on a fee basis. In essence, the service center rents computer time and provides related processing services. Tax service centers generally have a good reputation. While there have been major problems with software updates, on the whole, service centers have a reputation for good service, but at a cost.

The major advantages of a service center are the quality of support to the preparer (good manuals, high quality user service, updates prepared on a timely basis) and the completeness of the service (i.e., substantially all forms are supported). Typically the costs are variable; thus if you do not use it, you do not pay for the service. Much of the processing of the return is handled at the service center. The preparer does not have to incur the cost of copying, collating, or otherwise handling the forms. Typically a limited number of reruns are available at no additional cost. Thus, for a low volume return preparer, the cost is comparable or perhaps lower than for in-house processing.

The major disadvantage is lack of control by the preparer. The data must be delivered to the service center; thus, it is removed from the control of the preparer. The completed tax return must be returned to the preparer, which means that the turnaround time to complete a return is not controlled by the preparer. These problems have been addressed in several ways. First, the service centers typically allow preparers to input data electronically over data communication connections; thus, the input time has been reduced greatly. Also, the service center will typically process 24 hours a day, which also reduces the time required to process a return. Lastly, in larger cities, private carriers have been used to reduce the time for delivery of the completed return. The result of all these improvements has been overnight processing in major cities.

The major use of service centers is for the most complicated returns that a preparer prepares. Thus, the primary role of service centers in the mid 1990s is as a secondary source of preparation software. Some tax professionals believe that service centers will soon be obsolete due to the availability of in-house alternatives.

Mixed In-House and Service Center

The two methods discussed above have significant advantages and disadvantages. One solution to the problems has been to combine the two processing modes into a mixed in-house and service center processing. The typical procedure is similar to in-house processing; in fact, some users of the mixed mode believe that they are using complete in-house processing. The preparer will input the data using a desktop computer. The software will determine if the return can be processed locally or if the return requires a form that is not supported by the in-house software. If required, the software will connect electronically with the service center and the return will be processed there. The completed return will then be electronically sent to the preparer's computer and printed on the preparer's local printer. The preparer has complete control over the timing of the processing. While the data is still subject to going outside of the preparer's office, the turnaround problem is reduced. Also, the cost is variable; thus, it may be more expensive for a high volume tax return preparer than in-house processing. However, the mixed mode does allow the preparer to use a service center for the most complicated returns. Also, the service center support staff will be available to help with processing problems if needed. Again, if the days of service centers are numbered, then the mixed method may be quietly disappearing also.

Hardware and System Requirements

With the advances in personal computers and laser printers, many preparers are finding that the PC provides all the computer power necessary to process tax returns. Processing tax returns does require significant computations and is therefore impacted by the type of processor used in the personal computer. Also, because of the large number of MS-DOS personal computers in use, most software is written to use the Microsoft Windows 95 operating system. (The TurboTax for Windows version is included with this manual.) Thus, an IBM PC or IBM PC compatible personal computer is required for most tax return preparation software. However, if the number of Apple Macintosh PCs increases, the number of software packages written for the Macintosh will also increase. (TurboTax is available in a Macintosh version called MacInTax®.)

Tax software is computationally orientated, thus, the speed of its operation can be improved with a fast microprocessor such as Intel's Pentium and Pentium II microprocessors which include a math coprocessor to speed the mathematical computations. (A math coprocessor is not required with TurboTax.) If any services of a service center are to be used, the PC must be equipped with communication hardware (a serial port with an attached modem unless a digital phone system is used) and communication software. Also, communication hardware and software is needed if electronic filing is done or if you plan to use the Internet.

Most tax return preparation software is graphically oriented. When Microsoft Windows is used the software will display on the screen the tax return exactly as it will be printed. Color display is useful because some of the software products will highlight key parts of the tax form with color. Both graphic display and color requires a graphics card. While a monochrome (black & white, or green) display will work, it is not recommended. The use of a mouse interface is optional, but it is useful and strongly recommended. The mouse will especially be useful when using the TurboTax **EasyStep** method. If tax data are to be entered entirely from the keyboard and the **Forms Method** is used, the mouse is still useful to help you move between the various forms. Thus, use the mouse.

As we move further into the 1990s, the presence of Microsoft Windows has begun to dominate the market. Windows gives the user a graphical user interface, meaning that the screen consists of graphical images and data rather than character data alone. What you see on the screen is what will be printed. With tax preparation software, the result is that all forms and schedules look just like official IRS forms. This graphical user interface, first introduced by the Macintosh operating system, is the standard interface for business software.

The standard printer for use with professional tax return preparation software is a laser printer. While some software supports the use of a dot matrix printer (TurboTax for one), all software packages recommend a laser printer because of its high quality text and graphic output. It should be understood that all laser printers are not the same. Because of differences, software referred to as "printer drivers," must be available for your specific printer. As may be expected, all tax return preparation software supports (i.e. provides the driver, if necessary) the leading brands of printers. It is best to check the software manual or check with the vendor before purchasing a printer to insure that you will not have compatibility problems, especially if the market leader is not purchased. TurboTax supports a wide range of printers which most likely includes the one you are using. The potential problems of an incompatible printer is one reason for purchasing the market leader or a printer that is compatible. Most accountants use one of the several Hewlett Packard LaserJet printers.

Selecting a Software Package

The first step in determining the specific software package to use is to analyze the type of returns that are expected to be prepared. Without question, this can be a time consuming process, especially if it must be done manually. The AICPA Tax Division publication, *Automation of the Tax Practice of the 90s* provides excellent worksheets to prepare this analysis. Once the analysis is completed, the software products can be sorted into those that support the forms typically prepared and those that do not. One of the deciding factors in the selection of a specific software will be whether or not the software will prepare the state tax returns that are needed by the preparer. If the state return must be prepared manually, substantial productivity is lost.

Information on costs, capabilities and availability is published in the September edition of the *Journal of Accountancy* and the October editions of the *Journal of Taxation* and *Taxation For Accountants* each year. In addition, several reviews of software products are published by computer magazines such as *InfoWorld, PC World, PC Magazine* and others. Also, various accounting newsletters publish lists of software and number of users.

The primary use of such information is to identify an initial list of software products. The final decision will rest with the preparer. The primary factors to consider are:

- Are relevant state tax returns supported?
- Are most forms used by preparer supported by software?
- Is cost of software reasonable?
- Are updates prepared each year on a timely basis?
- Does the software developer provide support services needed (e.g. training, manuals, telephone support)?
- Does the software provide an interface with accounting software used by preparer's clients?
- Does the software provide on-line help in using software? in accessing tax reference materials? in referring to IRS instructions?

As a general guideline, it is always better to "Try it before you buy it." Most software vendors will provide low cost demo versions to a preparer in order to evaluate the product. If not, the preparer should go to a known user with sample tax data in hand, and try the product at the user's location. It is important that the preparer, not a vendor, select the software that is best for the returns to be prepared.

Software Media

One of the newer features of tax preparation software is a change in the software media. Software is commonly distributed on high density disks (3.5 inch, 1.4MB disk, or CD-ROM). CD-ROM disks generally provide space for 650 megabytes or more of data. For example, since 1992, Research Institute of America (RIA) has been distributing software on a CD-ROM disk. CD-ROMs are also provided by Inuit for all their products, and by RIA for Fast Tax (a competing professional tax preparation software package) and *OnPoint*, a widely-used electronic research tool. A web version of *OnPoint*, called *CheckPoint*, became available in 1997. The extra storage capacity on CD-ROMs enables storage of multimedia materials - such as video and audio clips providing tax and financial advice.

The cost of manufacturing a CD-ROM is about $800 for the master disk and less than $2 per copy. For the producer, this is less expensive than a set of floppy disks. CD-ROM and World Wide Web servers are becoming the primary storage media for all reference materials. In addition to RIA's product, CCH makes its well known *Access* reference materials available on CD-ROM and the web. Tax Analysts, an Alexandria, Virginia, publisher of tax materials including *Tax Notes*, makes original source documents like court cases, rulings and regulations available on CD-ROM media, called *InfoTax*. West Publishing Company also distributes its tax service *WestLaw* on CD-ROM. Thus, it is clear that the preferred storage media for reference materials in the 1990s is the CD-ROM and web servers. The combination of electronic tax research and tax preparation on one disk and/or via the web are becoming the standard.

CONCLUDING COMMENTS

The use of tax technology using the Windows operating system/environment by tax preparers is the current norm. The use of tax preparation software like TurboTax is required knowledge of tax return preparers. You have made a good choice in selecting this software. Good luck with your use of tax preparation software and in your career as a professional accountant.

CHAPTER 2

OVERVIEW OF TURBOTAX

Intuit Inc. supplies user-friendly business and accounting software and related products to three markets - individuals, businesses, and professional accountants. In the tax area, *TurboTax* is used for preparing personal tax returns (Form 1040) and *TurboTax for Business* prepares returns for regular corporations (Form 1120), S corporations (Form 1120S), partnerships and most limited liability companies (Form 1065), and sole proprietorships (Form 1040). *ProSeries* is designed for professional tax accountants. All *TurboTax* software operates on IBM PCs and compatibles. *MacInTax* is the Macintosh version of *TurboTax*. Users can acquire Intuit software on CD-ROM or on 3.5" diskettes. A downloadable state product is also available from the Inuit web site.

Other Intuit products include *Quicken* and *QuickBooks*. Very briefly, these packages perform a wide variety of personal finance and accounting functions including check-writing, checking account analysis, budgeting, payroll, and financial statement preparation. Users can electronically copy financial information from this software directly into Intuit tax software for tax return preparation.

To find out more about these and additional Intuit products, visit the Intuit web sites:

http://www.turbotax.com
http://www.intuit.com

READ THIS BEFORE YOU START

As mentioned above, TurboTax is designed to be used by taxpayers who prepare their own return. Accordingly, it is easy to use and includes a variety of sophisticated tools to help the user. The primary taxpayer aid is the EasyStep Interview, a comprehensive interactive interview that leads the user through the tax return preparation process. The EasyStep Interview is designed to ask all the right questions and to put your answers on the correct form. In the EasyStep Interview you can select the "Fast Track" option which allows you to customize the questions the EasyStep Interview asks. TurboTax also supports the Forms method which is a form oriented approach to tax preparation. Here you select the forms you want and enter the required information. Knowledge of tax return preparation is suggested to successfully use the Forms method. In addition, TurboTax has online help to aid you in using the software, online access to selected IRS Instructions, online TurboTax tax aids, and a variety of worksheets designed to reduce complex tax laws to easy-to-follow steps. The software operates in an intuitive manner with ample screen prompts. The use of a mouse and pull-down menus operate in a manner consistent with popular business software designed to run in the Windows environment. Accordingly, most tax students who use Windows based software find the menus both familiar and comfortable.

When using the EasyStep Interview, the software will make decisions about where to report your information based upon your answers. You will be able to see where TurboTax is entering your data because the form being used is displayed in the lower half of the screen. TurboTax makes all necessary computations automatically. One major difference between TurboTax and spreadsheet software like Lotus and Excel is that you will not be able to see the formulas used by TurboTax to make tax calculations.

Following the EasyStep Interview will result in a completed, correct tax return. Of course, as you gain experience, you can elect to bypass the EasyStep Interview and use the Forms method where you have much more control over the preparation of your return. However, your chances for making mistakes would increase.

Data Source is one of the help features. While using the Forms method, you can move the cursor to any field. Then, pressing the **right** button on your mouse will display a menu of which one option is **Data Source**. Selecting **Data Source** displays the source of any calculated amounts. TurboTax uses the term "calculated amounts" to refer to any data item that is either transferred from another location in TurboTax or is the result of a calculation on the current form. Also, if the field is a calculated amount, it will display a magnifying glass icon adjacent to the field. Clicking on the glass will move you to the form that is the source of the amount, i.e. the same information available by selecting **Data Source**. Thus, by using **Data Source** you can determine how the forms are interconnected, and by clicking on the magnifying glass icon, you can see those forms. Doing so will help you better understand the tax forms and how they are linked.

When using the Forms method, always begin with the Personal Information Worksheet. This is where you enter the taxpayer's name and other identifying information. At the bottom of the form, you double click to QuickZoom® to Form 1040. From there, move down Form 1040 to the line where your transaction is reported and go to the appropriate supporting statement by double clicking on that line. These methods are discussed more fully in the following chapters.

The purpose of this chapter is to describe how to install TurboTax and provide an overview on using the software. If you are new to both TurboTax and tax return preparation, the EasyStep method is strongly recommended. As you become more familiar with tax return preparation and with the software, you can elect to use the Forms method. The Forms method takes less time, but requires a higher level of knowledge. In this manual, Chapter 3 is a detailed explanation of how to use the EasyStep method, including how to minimize your data entry time using Fast Track. Chapter 4 covers the Forms method. Chapter 5 discusses how Intuit will help you use TurboTax and Chapter 6 includes problems to give you practice in using the software.

The topics discussed in this chapter are:

- Hardware Requirements for TurboTax
- How to install TurboTax using Windows 3.1
- How to install TurboTax using Windows 95
- Printing the Return
- Saving Taxpayer Data Files
- Quick Start to using the EasyStep method

THE READ1040 FILE IS IMPORTANT

Information about the software that became available after the manual was prepared is included in the file READ1040 on the CD-ROM. It is to your advantage to read this file prior to using TurboTax. READ1040 file is a "WRI" file that is associated with the Windows Accessory program *NotePad*. Thus, by listing the files on the floppy disk drive (A or B) using either File Manager (with Windows 3.1) or Windows Explorer (with Windows 95) and then double clicking the file name READ1040, you will load both NotePad and the READ1040 file. In NotePad you can read the contents of the file or print them. When using Windows 3.1, the readability will be enhanced if you select the EDIT command option, **Word Wrap**, prior to browsing the file. If you are using the Windows 95 version of *NotePad*, simply maximize the window and you will be able to read the entire text conveniently. After you install TurboTax, the READ1040 file will be automatically stored in the TAX97 subdirectory for future reference.

HARDWARE REQUIREMENTS

TurboTax for Windows will operate with just about any hardware configuration that is compatible with Windows. The minimum hardware required for **this version** is listed below.

1. IBM PC or a compatible with a 486 DX or higher processor and Windows 3.1, 95, or Windows for Workgroup.
2. At least 4 megabytes of RAM (8 megabytes recommended),
3. A hard (or fixed) disk with 24 megabytes of space available.

4. 2X CD-ROM drive.
5. Electronic filing and online features require a 9600 baud (or faster) modem, or direct connection via a LAN.
6. TurboTax supports most laser, inkjet and dot-matrix printers.
7. A standard color VGA monitor with a minimum of 256 colors available.

In addition, TurboTax for Windows works better with a mouse and one is strongly recommended. The use of a modem is supported for electronic filing, which is the future of tax preparation. As indicated above, TurboTax will work with 4 megs of RAM. However, note that all Windows programs, including TurboTax, work **better** with 8 or more megs of RAM. Any new PC purchased in 1998 should have at least **16 megs** of RAM to efficiently run Windows software.

The end product of tax return preparation software is a filed tax return, normally printed. TurboTax produces its best output with a laser printer. However, in an educational environment, laser printers are not always available. For academic purposes, a 100 percent compatible Epson or IBM 9 or 24 pin dot matrix printer is acceptable -- TurboTax supports a long list of both laser printers and dot matrix printers. Before printing you must specify the type of printer you are using with the Print Manager, a part of the Windows Control Panel menu. The only problem with using dot matrix printers is the speed of printing. Since this Windows version is graphical, all forms are printed in graphics mode; i.e., the dot matrix printer basically prints one row of dots at a time. Thus, printing with a dot matrix printer will be **very slow**. Be patient.

For more information about printing, refer to the **File Print** command discussed in Chapter 4.

INSTALLATION OF TURBOTAX

There are two sets of installation instructions -- one for Windows 3.1 and a second set for Windows 95. Follow the installation steps for the version of Windows that you use. Once you get the program installed, it works the same with either operating system/environment, though the screen will look different. Screens in this manual are based upon Windows 95. If you are using Windows 3.1, your screen will look different, but the commands will be the same.

To Install TurboTax for Windows 3.1

1. Turn on your computer. Load Windows if it is not loaded upon booting. To load Windows, enter **Win** at the DOS prompt.

2. Do not close Windows itself, but close all Windows programs (e.g., Word, Excel) as well as any non-Windows programs. As a precaution, it is recommended that you also close virus protection software.

3. Insert the TurboTax CD-ROM into your drive.

4. Select Windows' **File Manager** from the Main Program Group. Click on the CD-ROM disk icon (disk B, C, or D, etc.) to display its files.

5. Double-click on file **SETUP.EXE** to begin the installation process. The first screen of the TurboTax Installation menu will be displayed on the screen as shown in Figure 2-1, below.

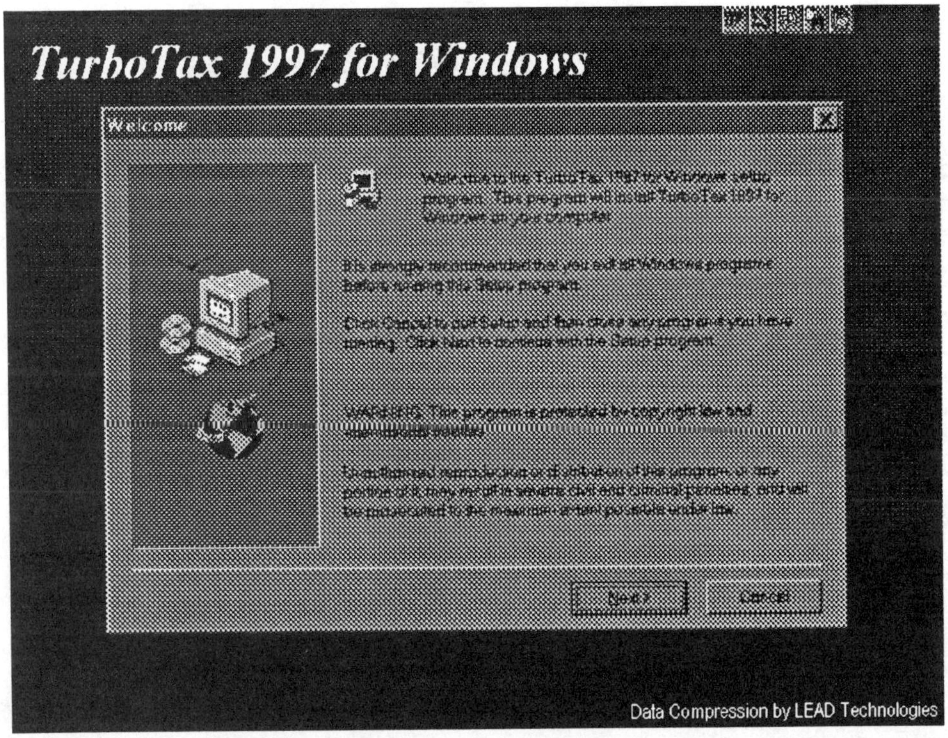

Figure 2-1 Welcome to the Installation Program

6. A "wizard" included on the CD-ROM will guide you through all installation steps. Just follow instructions on the screen. Among the TurboTax icons created during this process is an uninstall icon. You can click on this icon any time in the future to uninstall TurboTax.

7. To proceed from screen to screen, click on the Next button (or the Yes button). Read each screen. Several screens provide interesting information about TurboTax and other Intuit products. The installation process takes several minutes. Please be patient.

8. The setup program creates the Program Group "TurboTax 1997," three program items and their related icons, similar to those shown below.

Figure 2-2 Program Group icons

The red, white and blue top hat is the icon for TurboTax for Windows. The READ1040 icon displays information about the latest changes in the program. The Uninstall icon allows you to remove TurboTax from your disk after you have completed this course and do not expect to be using it again soon.

9. Once TurboTax is installed, the window shown below will appear. Click on OK and then double-click on the TurboTax icon to launch it.

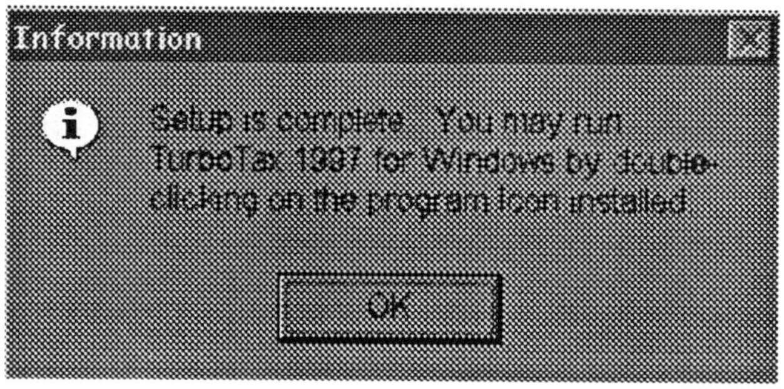

Figure 2-3 Information Box

10. At this point you have successfully installed TurboTax. If not, refer to the section, "What if My Software Won't Install?," for suggestions.

11. Once installed, TurboTax is ready to launch. One approach is to refer to the Quick Start section at the end of this chapter and start working problem 1 in Chapter 6. However, the recommended way to learn TurboTax is to read Chapter 3 on Using the EasyStep method before you start working problems.

To Install TurboTax for Windows 95

1. Turn on your computer. Sit back and wait until the boot-up process is complete.

2. Do not close Windows itself, but close all Windows programs (e.g., Word, Excel) as well as any non-Windows programs. As a precaution, it is recommended that you also close virus protection software.

3. Insert the TurboTax CD-ROM into your drive.

4. Click on the Start button located in the bottom left-hand corner of your screen. In the pop-up menu that appears, click on "Run ..." A "Run" dialog box will open, as shown below. If your CD-ROM drive is the d: drive, then in the input section in the middle of the dialog box, enter the following and then click OK   d:setup

   If your CD-ROM drive is other than the d: drive, just use the appropriate letter in place of "d".

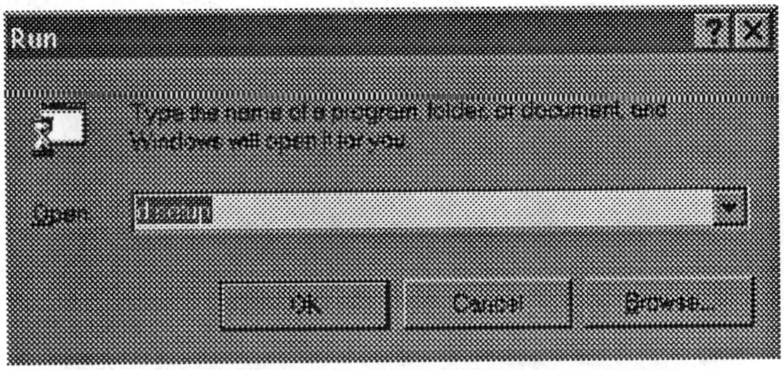

Figure 2-4 Run Dialog Box

5. A "wizard" included on the CD-ROM will guide you through all installation steps. Just follow te instructions on the screen. Among the TurboTax icons created during this process is an Uninstall icon. You can click on this icon anytime in the future to uninstall TurboTax.

6. To proceed from screen to screen, click on the Next button (or the Yes button). Read each screen. Several screens provide interesting information about TurboTax and other Intuit products. The installation process takes several minutes. Please be patient.

7. The setup program creates the Program Group "TurboTax 1997," three program items and their related icons, similar to those shown below.

Figure 2-5 Program Group icons

The red, white and blue top hat is the icon for TurboTax for Windows. The READ1040 icon displays information about the latest changes in the program. The Uninstall icon allows you to remove TurboTax from your disk after you have completed this course and do not expect to be using it again in the near term.

8. Once TurboTax is installed, the window shown below will appear. Click on OK and then double-click on the TurboTax icon to launch it.

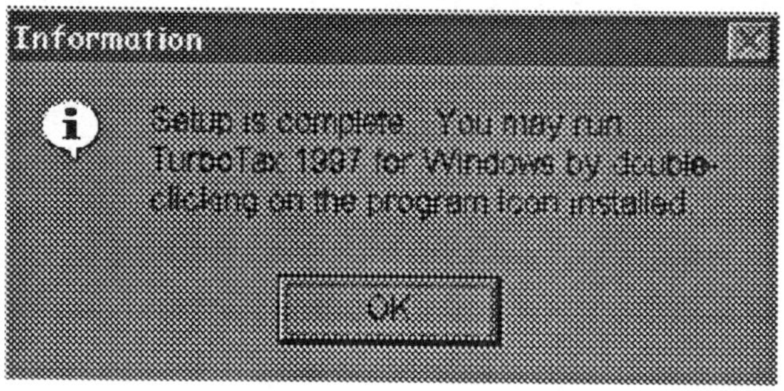

Figure 2-6 Information Box

9. At any time in the future, you can access TurboTax icons by first clicking on the Start button (located in the bottom left-hand corner of your screen). Then, click on the Program button. Finally, click on TurboTax.

10. If you receive a message that TurboTax did NOT install properly, refer to the section below, "What if My Software Won't Install?"

11. Once installed, you are ready to go. If you can wait no longer, refer to the Quick Start section at the end of this chapter and start working Problem 1 in Chapter 6. If you can spare the time, I suggest that you read Chapter 3 on Using the EasyStep method and Chapter 4 on Using the Forms Method before you start working problems.

What If My Software Won't Install?

You are likely reading this section because TurboTax did not install properly. First, rethink your steps. Did you miss one? For example, did you disable all virus-protection utilities and memory resident programs? Did you restart your PC after doing so?

Another problem can be space on your disk drive. If your hard disk is small by today's standards, this is a major problem for all Windows software. You need at least 30 megabytes of space on your hard drive to load TurboTax. If you are using DOS 6.2, you might try Double Space. If you are using Windows 95, you might try DriveSpace. I have used both (plus Stacker) and have had no problems. They nearly double the amount of software you can store on your disk. You may have to erase some other software to make room.

The TurboTax Setup program installs TrueType fonts needed by TurboTax. If you receive an error message indicating that it could not install these fonts, you must install them manually by following the instructions in your Windows User Guide. Check the Printer Manager.

QUICK START TO USING TURBOTAX

You have the software installed. If you are using Windows 3.1, you have a program group named "TurboTax 1997." If you are using Windows 95, you have a similar folder of programs that will be labeled "TurboTax 1997." With either software, you select the program group or folder, click on TurboTax 1997 and then click on the red, white and blue hat icon to load TurboTax for Windows into RAM. You will see a "Welcome to TurboTax" screen. Review your welcome. After you are done reading your welcome, click **Next**.

By default you are put in the **EasyStep** Interview, which is the easy way to go. As we have said before, for your first return, I suggest (urge) that you use the EasyStep method. While it will take you more time, TurboTax will walk you through the entire tax return preparation process. For your first return, do not select the **Fast Track** -- do the whole thing. The EasyStep method is an interview program that asks you tax questions in plain English and, based upon your answers, decides which tax forms you need, does all the calculations, and fills in the forms for you. Your part is to read the screen before you press the enter key or click the mouse. If you read the screen, you will prevent most common errors. For more information, read Chapter 3, Using the EasyStep method.

If you decide to use the Forms method, read Chapter 4.

In using the EasyStep method, one of the last steps is to "Review Your Return." The purpose of selecting this step is to allow TurboTax to check your return for errors. The program can not detect data entry errors, but it can check for errors of omission and illogical entries. Thus, if you check the "Single" filing status but you are married, TurboTax will not detect it. But, if you have checked Single and then attempt to enter a name for your spouse, TurboTax will give you an error message. Reviewing your return is a good thing and you should do it, every time.

PRINTING THE RETURN

The final step is to print the tax return. Before you print the tax return, however, you must inform TurboTax what printer you will be using. By default, TurboTax selects the printer you installed with Windows. That is, it uses the Windows Print Manager to do printing. If you are still using the same printer, you do not need to set up the printer again. If necessary to change the selected printer, go to the Print Manager in Windows and change your printer. You can change the option at any time by simply repeating the process. If your specific printer is not on the list, select one that is compatible to it. Changing the printer will normally not be required. The problem can arise if you are using a lab with a variety of printers and no lab monitor to keep the PCs correctly installed.

You print your return on plain white paper by selecting the **File Print** command or the **Filing** option in the EasyStep method. Note that you also have options to print Selected Forms, for example Form 1040, all forms, all worksheets, or all forms and worksheets -- "the whole thing." You can also print multiple copies of your return. You make your selection and click "Print" to continue. The first time you print, you should test-print one form to see if you have your printer correctly installed. If your printer is not selected correctly, you will know it immediately. Check your printer configuration and try again.

SAVING FILES IN TURBOTAX

You can save as many files in the current directory as you desire. Also, you select the filename. TurboTax adds the filetype "TAX," but you can identify the return anyway you desire. I suggest that you use some part of the taxpayer's name. For example when you do Mary Brown's return in Chapter 6, I suggest that you use the name "MBROWN" as your file name. At the time you save the file, you will have to specify the desired directory if you want to save the file in another directory. For example, if you wanted to save MBROWN on a floppy disk in the A drive, you would specify the file name as **A:\MBROWN**. The actual filename will be "MBROWN.TAX" and you will be able to find it when you use the **File Open** option. The file contains only the data; none of the form itself is saved with the data. When you open the file, data is added to the appropriate forms throughout in the program.

TURBOTAX HELP

Help with TurboTax is available in different forms. First, Chapters 3 and 4 of this manual can act as a reference. Each command is discussed, including both how to use the command and when it should be used. Second, TurboTax has an extensive online Help function that is designed to give you online assistance while you operate the program. Help is selected from the main menu or from the Help button displayed with the forms. Also, several features of TurboTax are designed to help you complete the return. These help features are discussed below.

EasyStep Interview -- This option is an interactive question and answer format that is designed to help you identify and complete the correct forms. (Note, it can be selected when you first enter TurboTax, or later after you have completed part of the return using the Forms methods.) If you want to take a break and return to the forms later, TurboTax will remember where you left off and put you in that same location the next time you load TurboTax.

Under Tools, Final Review -- Did you forget something? Most likely yes. Options under this command will remind you of your errors -- something like a professor or a spouse. For example, if you forget to answer all the questions at the bottom of Schedule B, selecting Review will remind you to answer all such questions.

Tax help -- This options tells you how to enter information in the currently displayed form, and explains what TurboTax does with the information you enter. It is context sensitive, thus TurboTax interprets the current field on the tax form and provides the help needed.

Data Source -- This selection lists the **source** of the information that TurboTax transfers to the current line of the tax form which is marked with the cursor.

Government (IRS) Instructions -- This selection causes TurboTax to display the IRS instructions for the form shown on the screen. With the state version of TurboTax, the government instructions are those of that state. For a New York return, the IRS instructions would be of limited use.

Program Help -- Should you need help understanding how TurboTax itself works, select this help tab.

In Chapter 5, the help available directly from the Intuit Customer Service support group is discussed. There, the telephone numbers for the various kinds of help are listed. Intuit is committed to supporting you even though your software was purchased from South-Western College Publishing.

TURBOTAX ON THE WORLD WIDE WEB

For more information about Intuit products, including TurboTax, see their sites on the World Wide Web at the following URLs:

http://www.turbotax.com
http://www.intuit.com

You must have your own browser software. If you do not have a browser, use the Microsoft Internet Explorer included in this package and take a look at the web.

The TurboTax web site is available 24-hours a day, seven days a week. In this time of changing tax laws, it is good to have a source that is committed to keeping you up-to-date on law changes.

CONCLUDING COMMENTS

Our purpose here was to help you install TurboTax for Windows and to give you a brief overview of how it works. If you are experienced using Windows software and using a mouse, you should be able to load the software and follow the on-screen instructions. As with any new software, you need to have the mind set of try and try again. Computers do not get upset if you make an error, so why should you? Simply press the ESC key or click on **Cancel**, and try it again.

If you are an experienced Windows user, you are ready to get started. If you follow your instincts and expect the keys to work in TurboTax like the keys function in other Windows software, you will not be disappointed. The following chapters cover the commands and their use. I hope that you find it useful to read the entire manual; however, the primary use of these later chapters is as a reference manual -- Chapter 3 for the EasyStep method, and Chapter 4 for the Forms method. Good Luck!

CHAPTER 3

USING THE EASYSTEP METHOD

Once you have TurboTax installed you are ready to complete a return. TurboTax provides two approaches to completing a tax return: 1 the **EasyStep Method** and 2 the **Forms Method**. Use of the Forms Method is discussed in Chapter 4. Here we discuss the EasyStep Method. As the name implies, this approach to completing a tax return is easy to do, although it can take more time to complete. Because of its ease of use, I urge you to try it the easy way before you tackle the Forms Method.

The EasyStep Method is an interview that turns your tax return into a series of simple steps. TurboTax walks you through your transactions in a question/answer format. TurboTax provides the questions in simple English; you provide the answers. Then TurboTax takes your answers and places them on the appropriate line on the correct form. The numbers are added; the totals transferred from the detailed worksheets and forms to the summary forms. Along the way, the "Tax Advisor" feature makes suggestions regarding your answers. In some cases the “Tax Advisor” will make a selection for you based upon generally accepted tax planning. For example, if you specify that you are preparing a return for a married couple, the “Tax Advisor” will elect the filing status, Married Filing Jointly. Normally, this is the correct option. Of course, you can change any selection made by the advisor. When you have finished your interview, TurboTax checks for missing information, and then tells you how to print the return. That's all there is to it. Of course if you answer the questions incorrectly, errors will occur. It is very important in using the EasyStep Method to read the screen before you press enter or click on the mouse.

TO BEGIN -- LOAD THE SOFTWARE

While the terminology is different between Windows 95 and Windows 3.1, the method of loading the software is the same. You simply point at the icon and click on the mouse. More specifically, in Windows 95, you execute the following steps:

1. Click on the "Start" icon.

2. Move the mouse pointer to the "Programs," then to the "TurboTax" folder title and then to "TurboTax for Windows 1997" with the red, white and blue TurboTax for Windows icon. Once the pointer is pointing to TurboTax, click your mouse.

3. TurboTax is loaded. You are immediately welcomed and invited to click on the "Next" button. TurboTax is ready for you to get started.

If you are using Windows 3.1, follow these steps:

1. Double-click on the icon for the TurboTax for Windows program group.

2. Point to the red, white and blue TurboTax icon and double-click.

3. TurboTax is loaded. You are immediately welcomed and invited to click on the "Next" button. TurboTax is ready for you to get started.

Click on the **Next** button in the lower right hand corner. Your first decision comes when you are told to that you have "Two Ways to Do Your Taxes." Figure 3-1 is a screen print showing the options. The choices are "1. The EasyStep Method," or "2. Forms Method." In this chapter, the focus is on the EasyStep Method; the following chapter discusses the Forms Method.

Select the EasyStep Method by clicking on Next button in the lower right hand corner of the highlighted window. To select the Forms Method, click on the small oval icon in the lower right hand corner of the screen labeled "Go to Forms." You get the idea that TurboTax wants you to use the EasyStep Method, and for now that is a good idea. So here we are going to talk about The EasyStep Method.

BASICS OF THE EASYSTEP INTERVIEW

The EasyStep Method is built on an easy-to-use Interview format. *Money* magazine periodically reviews the leading personal tax return preparation software packages. According to *Money*, ". . . all of the top programs use the approach pioneered by TurboTax: an automated interview in which your PC asks you a long list of tax-related questions and fills in the appropriate lines on the forms." Interview is the focus of the EasyStep Method and when you use it, you will see why others praise it so.

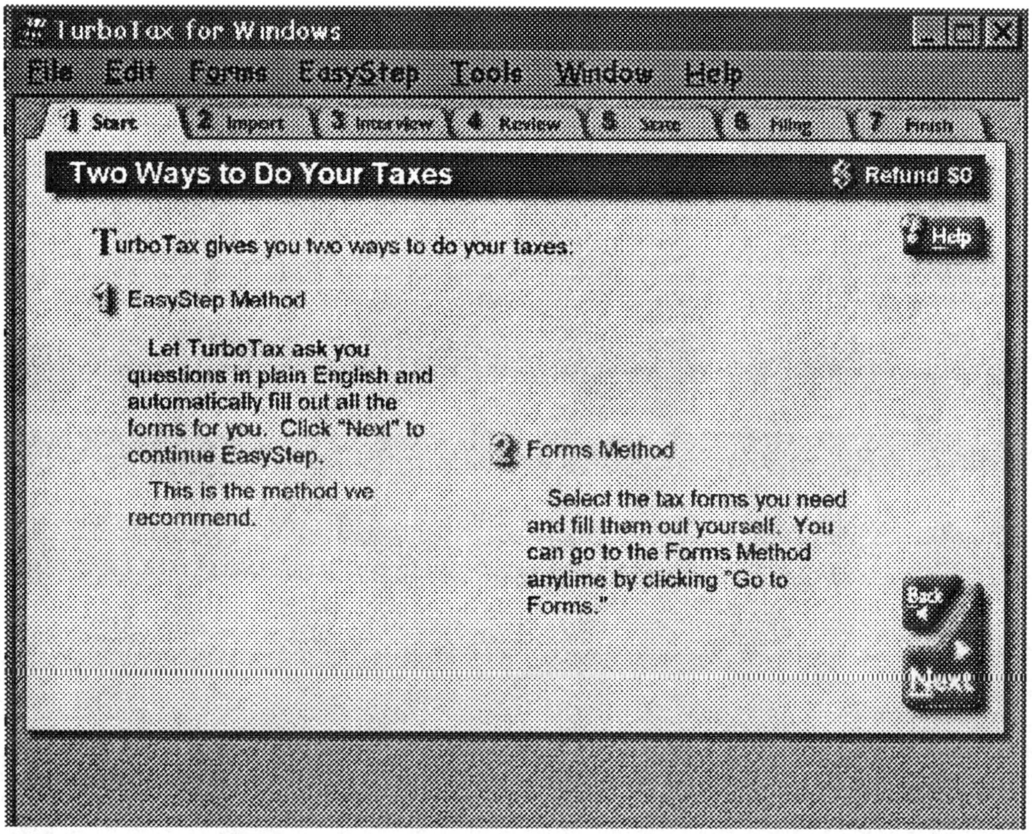

Figure 3-1 The EasyStep Method or Forms Method - You Choose

Figure 3-2 shows the standard screen for the EasyStep Method. Begin at the top. Windows uses the top roll of the screen to display the file name and program currently running. TurboTax takes over and uses the second row of the screen to list the TurboTax commands. While using the EasyStep Method, you will rarely use these commands -- the EasyStep Method uses these commands when it is appropriate. Thus, while in the EasyStep Interview, ignore these commands. The next row shows the tabs for the seven steps of the EasyStep Interview. These steps are: Start, Import, Interview, Review, State, Filing, Finish.

Detailed information about these steps is provided later. For now, look at the other parts of the screen. The area under the tab is called the "Dialog Area." Here is where you and TurboTax talk to each other. Note in Figure 3-2, the dialog area is labeled "Using the Interview." The label gives you an idea of the purpose of the dialog area. On the right side of the label bar, TurboTax displays the "bottom line" of your tax return, that is the amount of your "Refund" or "Amount Due." In Figure 3-2, the Refund is $0. Thus, you can look at the effect of each transaction on the bottom line as you enter the tax item. In the right part of the dialog area are three buttons that are displayed as long as you are using the EasyStep Method. The top button is a small question mark imposed on an oval containing the word "Help." This is the icon for accessing the TurboTax help feature. Help provides you a wealth of information about both the tax law and how to use TurboTax. Below the Help icon are the Back or Next buttons. (Note in Figure 3-2, the Next button is not available for this screen -- you have to select the button "Tell how this works" or "Let's get started." These buttons are the primary movement button for the EasyStep Method. They refer to going forward to the next screen or backward to the previous screen. (Bet you are wondering how I figured that out!) At the very bottom of the screen, on the right, you will see the "Go To Forms" button. It is purposely small so you will not hop to the forms and leave the EasyStep Method until you are ready. You should do at least two returns using the EasyStep Method before you move to the forms. The Forms Method is discussed in Chapter 4.

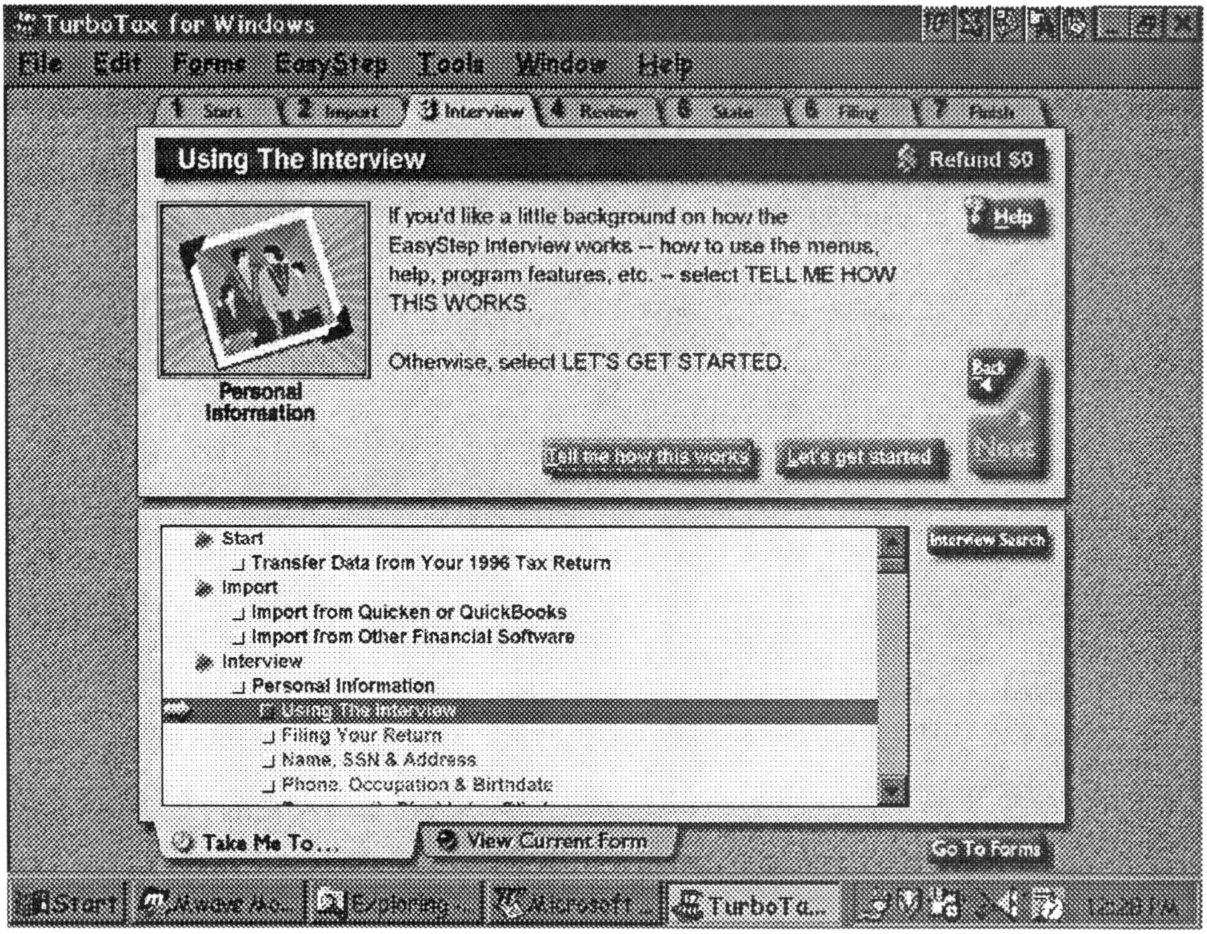

Figure 3-2 The EasyStep Method Screen

Because of its great usefulness to most of us, I want to add a bit about the Help feature. TurboTax does a good job of giving you the information you need when you need it. In other words, the help function is context sensitive. There are four types of help available and these are listed below.

- 1. Program Help — Explains Turbo Tax features including much of what is in this manual, but it is online; this manual is on paper.

- 2. Tax Help — These tax aids explain tax forms and tax items in "plain English" and give you tips about where on the form to report the items.

- 3. Government Instructions — The details of tax preparation are in the IRS Instructions. They are provided in convenient online screens. You will learn a lot by taking the time to read several of these screens.

- 4. Data Source — Did you ever use a software package and wonder, "Where did that number come from?" Well, TurboTax tells you with its Data Source help feature. Many of the numbers on a tax return are transferred from other forms. TurboTax also uses many worksheets to perform preliminary calculations. It shows you the source of these transferred amounts. When you are wondering, "Where did that come from?" click on Data Source to find out. Data Source is available on the forms directly or can be selected as one of the Help options.

That is the standard screen. Note in Figure 3-2, the "Next" button is gray or shaded. This means that it is not available at this time. That means that you have to click elsewhere to move forward. In Figure 3-2, you have to choose between the "Tell me how this works" or "let's get started" buttons to move. The "Tell me .." button moves you to a short tutorial on the EasyStep Method. I suggest you take the time to go through this tutorial. It will be worth it. The focus in using the EasyStep Method is the seven steps that have a tab at the top of the screen. Let's take a closer look at these.

1 Start

Starting has to be the easiest of the easy steps. You are asked if you used TurboTax last year. Most of you did not, thus you answer No and TurboTax will check off the only step in Start. If you used TurboTax last year, you would have been guided to transfer the carryover data from your 1996 tax return to the 1997 return. Here is one of the real powers of using tax preparation software. When you transfer last year's data forward, you save significant data entry. Data such as your name, address, sources of income, listed deductions, depreciation schedules, and so on are added to your current year return. The data that changes between years, such as dollar amounts of income, will not be transferred, but all that text data will hop right in. It is great!

One additional note. Because TurboTax is designed for individual taxpayers who typically file only one return, it expects that you will complete only your own personal tax return. Thus, after you complete or simply work on a return, that last return worked on will automatically be loaded when you start TurboTax. For the second and later returns, you will have to select the File command, **New Tax Return** to get started. You will be given an opportunity to save the existing return that is about to be closed.

You should save it. After you have told TurboTax that you are ready to start and that you will not be transferring any data from last year, you move to the second step.

2 Import

Import allows you to link with various financial software, such as Quicken and QuickBooks developed by Intuit. You will likely not need to use this feature in your tax course.

3 Interview

As you most likely expect, here is where you do the work of completing the return. The look of the screen changes. You will see the form or worksheet being completed at the bottom of the screen with a dialog box in the top half of the screen. (See Figure 3-2.) Once you pass the initial screens, you will see that in the dialog box you are asked a question. Then your response becomes an entry on the form or worksheet displayed at the bottom of the screen. Being able to see the destination of your entry reduces the "black box" feeling when using the EasyStep Method.

Take Me To...

Note in Figure 3-2, that the bottom dialog box has two tabs at the bottom of the box. The "Take Me To..." Tab is active in Figure 3-2. When active, all of the steps are listed with a scroll bar at the right so that you can move throughout the steps. Using this option allows you to speed up the Interview. Thus, if you know that you do not have any wages and salary reported on Form W-2 nor any interest or other income reported on Form 1099, you can scroll down to the Business Income, Schedule C line and enter the Interview at that location. Thus, you can use the EasyStep Method even if you do feel that you have a good understanding of what forms you will need.

The second bottom tab, "View Current Form," will display the form where the data you are entering will be placed. See Figure 3-3.

Fast Track

Fast Track is a streamlined interview option that allows users to select specific topics on which to be interviewed. The goal is to give you all the help you need, but to not force you to read through questions that do not relate to your return. For your first return, I urge you to take the "Entire Course" and read all the questions. While you will answer "No" to many of them, you will learn a great deal about the types of income items and deduction items that are available. For your second return, I suggest that you try the Fast Track.

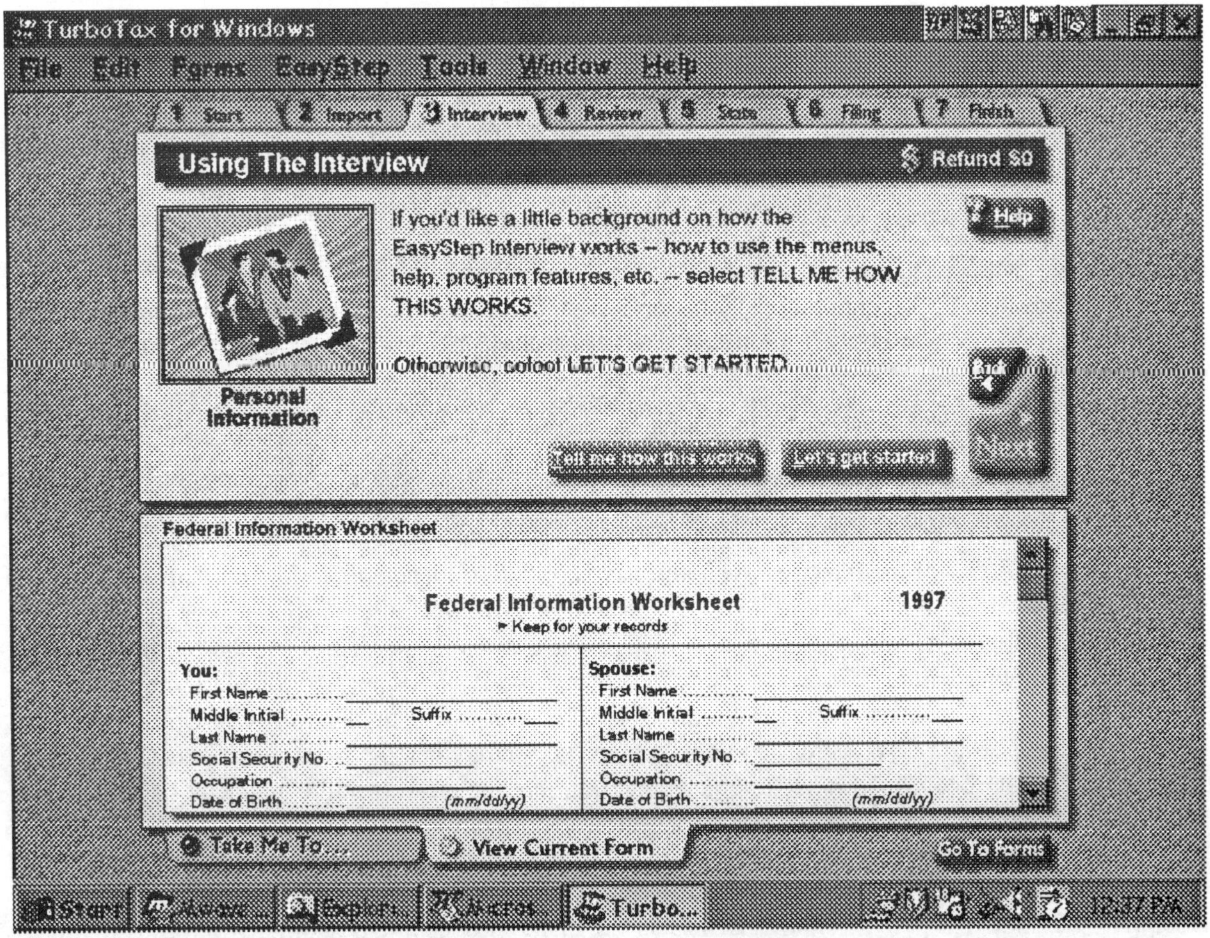

Figure 3-3 View Current Form Screen

The Interview Screens

As you go through the Interview screens you will see two basic types of screens. One will ask you to input data in data entry boxes. Note in the top dialog box are the data entry boxes. TurboTax will move you through each in the order of left to right and top to bottom. As you enter data, it is placed on the appropriate line on the form displayed in the lower half of the screen. Note if you have selected "Take Me To..." the bottom box does not display the form. Select "View Current Form" and you will see the form. Refer to Figure 3-3.

The second basic form of Interview screens is the question/answer format. Here TurboTax asks objective, "Yes/No" closed end questions. You answer by pointing to your answer with the mouse and clicking. TurboTax will normally suggest an answer, the default answer, indicated by a dotted-line box around the answer. If the default answer is acceptable, you may press the enter key to select it and move on. You can select any answer by pointing to the answer and clicking the mouse once.

At times you will be given the option of answering the question directly or getting additional help. For example, you can select the filing status directly by pointing to one of the alternative statuses. Alternatively, you can select an option "Guide Me," and TurboTax will go through the requirements for each status and select, based upon your answers, the appropriate status. Thus, you have alternative levels of support available.

Leftovers?

If, after the completion of the Interview, you still have an item of income or deduction that you have not considered, you can use the "Take Me To..." option and look over the all the various types of income and deductions. If that is not successful, click on **Help** and then on "Tax Help". At the top of the dialog box, is a row of four buttons: Go Back, Search, Contents, Print. Selecting the Search button opens the "Help Topics" search window shown in Figure 3-4. This window is similar to a File Open window in most Windows software. To search for your leftover tax item, enter the name of the item in block 1. Describe it in general terms, such as "mortgage interest," not the more specific "payment of interest and principal." As you type in the name, TurboTax automatically moves through the list of terms searching for your term. If it finds it, you can click on the "Display" button. You will open a window with an explanation of the item and information about where to report the item. In the discussion, some of the items may be underlined. If so, you can click on the underlined item and additional information about that item will be displayed. You can click on the print button to send the information to the printer.

To close the help, click on the X in the upper right hand corner on the "Search Topics" bar, or click on the "Close" button in the lower right corner of the screen. If you click on the top most X, you will exit TurboTax. I do not think you want to do that here. You will be asked to save the file if you do click on the wrong X. Given the option to save, I urge you to take it. If you say no, you will still exit the program and you will lose any data not previously saved. Not a good thing. If you should exit, simply reload TurboTax. You will be returned to the last file you worked on and at the location you stopped working. Thus, you can easily get back to where you were.

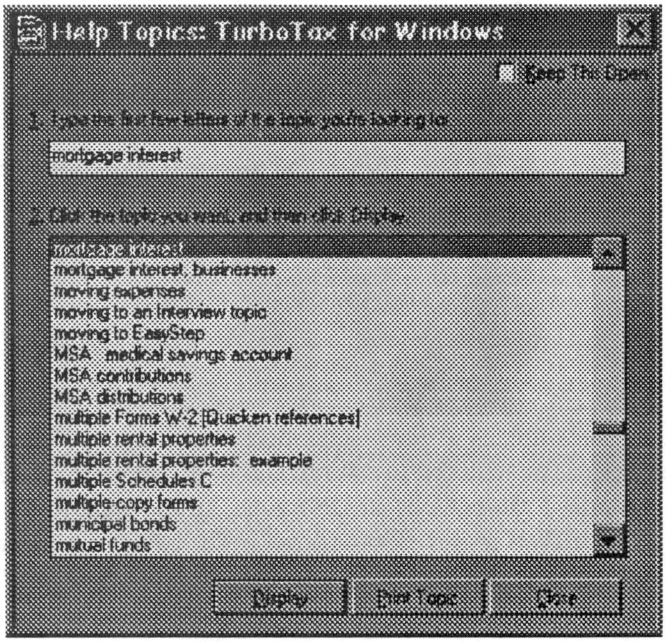

Figure 3-4 Help Topics

4 Review

With the interview completed, the tax return should be completed. TurboTax provides a module that allows you to check the return for errors. TurboTax conducts the following types of reviews:

1. Error Check -- contradictory or missing entries.
2. Deduction Finder -- deductions you may have overlooked.
3. Audit Alerts -- situations that might provoke an IRS audit or inquiry. These suggestions are based upon norms for given income levels.
4. U.S. Averages Comparison — Your tax return items will be compared in columnar format with the average items for a taxpayer with similar adjusted gross income. The purpose of the comparison is just for your information. While it is true that the IRS audit selection programs use this type of information to select returns for audit, your goal is to prepare a return that is correct. Thus, the probability of an audit is not relevant to you. At least, it should not be relevant.
5. Tax Report -- a printable plan of action and tips to help save on next year's taxes.

The results of Audit Flags, Tax Savings Ideas, and Deductions Finder reviews are for information only; no changes are required. When you reach the **Review** step, you will have the option of selecting any or all of the above four types of reviews. You simply click on the box next to the type of review. For the first few returns, I suggest that you select all Reviews so that you will be familiar with the type of information available.

Generally, you will discover that you failed to check a required box or to provide some other required information. In the EasyStep Method you will be led to the interview step where the error is addressed and given an opportunity to correct the error. The instructions will be displayed on the screen, so all you have to do is click on the **Next** button and read the screen. The items identified by the **Review** step are listed one problem at a time, in a dialog box. When you are using the Forms Method, you can click on the Forms Menu Option, Form Errors. TurboTax moves you to the appropriate line on the appropriate form where you can edit the line to fix the problem.

5 State

In the real world, most of you will have to file a state income tax return. Typically, for class purposes you do not complete the associated state return. With TurboTax, the state return is a separate module and is not available from South-Western College Publishing. If you want to purchase the state module, check Intuit on the World Wide Web or call 1-800-4-Intuit. The state module works in the same way as the federal module. The degree of integration is wonderful. Intuit has done a good job of making completing the state return easy.

6 Filing

Tax returns are normally filed on paper. To file on paper you need to print your return. With the EasyStep Method, you will just select the "Print conventional Format" button and sit back and watch. TurboTax will print the entire form, with all of the supporting schedules. If you want more control over what you print, select the File Print command from the File menu. You are presented with a dialog box in which you can make several elections. You are able to print the entire return or portions of the return. You can specify the number of copies you want and you can specify the order of printing, i.e. front to back or back to front. The correct order depends upon how your printer outputs paper, i.e. face up or face down. If face down, select "front to back." The worst that can happen is that you will have to shuffle the forms to get the correct order. Normally printing is a breeze. In chapter 4, under the discussion of the Print command, I give you more information for those times when everything goes wrong.

An option selected as you complete the Federal Information Worksheet is to print the return in the Form 1040PC-format. Form 1040PC returns are condensed to three columns per page. This format takes far less paper than the conventional format. See Figure 3-5 PC Format. You can still select it from the File Print menu option or the Filing tab,. A Form 1040PC-format return is only created after you complete the return. It really is just a print option and not an alternative to the Form 1040. Most returns can be printed in no more than 2 pages if the 1040PC format is selected. Check with your professor to see if he or she wishes you to submit returns formatted as 1040PCs. If so you will save a great deal of printing time and paper.

Increasingly the IRS is making it possible to file your return electronically, "the way of the future." In fact by the year 2001, electronic filing is predicted to be the preferred choice of most taxpayers. If you have a refund due or a zero-balance return that meets IRS requirements, a taxpayer can file electronically through the Intuit Electronic Filing Center -- they have good credit. To reach the Electronic Filing Center, you send your return via modem to Intuit. Then for a small fee ($9.95) Intuit sends the form electronically to the IRS. Currently the IRS insists upon a middle man because it lacks the hardware to handle the number of filers if each taxpayer could file directly to the IRS electronically. The GAO has been very critical of this policy. Anyway, for academic purposes, filing will consist of submitting a return to your instructor and normally it will be on paper. Thus, you will not use this option. Again, the PC format will save paper — I urge you to suggest it to your professor.

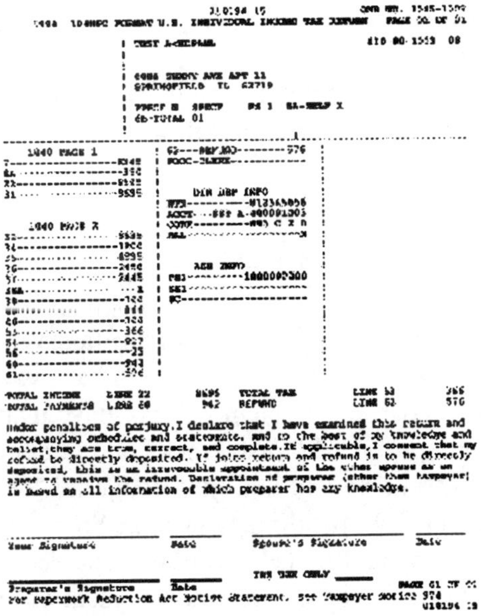

Figure 3-5 PC Format

7 Finish

All good things come to an end. This is also true of the preparation of a tax return. Once you have completed this year's return, it is time to start looking to next year. The **Finish** tab tells you that you can use the TurboTax W-4 Worksheet and Estimated Tax Worksheet in connection with the remaining months of the current tax year. Just click on "Help" to for more information about these features.

That is all there is to using the EasyStep Method. It is, as its name implies, easy to use. Note that you can leave the EasyStep Method at any point and move to the Forms Method by simply clicking on the *Go To Forms* icon. Also, you can take a break, exit TurboTax, and return later to the same step in the EasyStep Interview where you left off preparing the return. That is, when you reload TurboTax, you will be put at the same step and in the same file that was current when you exited TurboTax.

For an example of the use of the EasyStep Method to complete a return, the first problem in Chapter 6 is worked using the EasyStep Method approach and several screens for that problem are included there.

CONCLUDING COMMENTS

The EasyStep Interview is designed to be used by the normal taxpayer. Certainly, you have more tax training than the normal taxpayer. The problem I expect you to have with the EasyStep Method is having the patience to complete all steps. Your tax problem will not have many of the transactions included in the Interview. Recall that you can opt for the "Fast Track" and minimize the redundancy. In any case, for the first tax return, I urge you to be patient and go through all the questions. As you do, read the screens. If you read the screens, you will avoid many errors. Some of the problems you will work will have difficult tax issues, issues for which little help will be available from the online helps. Recall that you also have a tax textbook to search for the correct tax treatment of many transactions. First focus on determining the appropriate income, then the deductions. Use the Review step as a check. After you make corrections, review it again just to make certain.

Good Luck!

CHAPTER 4

USING THE FORMS METHOD

The EasyStep Method discussed in Chapter 3 provides you with an interview that takes your answers to questions and puts the information on the appropriate form. As you become more familiar with the forms and the required information, it will be obvious to you that the EasyStep Method takes more time than the Forms Method discussed here. If you know which form to use and understand the response needed for the form, it will be faster to go to the correct form and fill it out. The Forms Method is designed to let you do just that.

WHERE TO BEGIN

As part of the introduction screens, you have to select either the EasyStep Method or the Forms Method. (See Figure 3-1.) To select the Forms Method, you click on the *Go To Forms* icon, the blue oval icon in the lower right hand corner of the screen. When you double click on the icon, TurboTax moves you to the Federal Information Worksheet. All identifying information is entered on this worksheet. It tells TurboTax who you are and what preferences you have. For example, this is the worksheet where you will enter your name and address and indicate your preferences for filing, the Presidential Election Campaign Fund and other choices you have.

One item on the Federal Information Worksheet asks you to check a block in order to file the return in the 1040PC format. When you check the block, TurboTax will prepare your return in the PC format. For classroom purposes, ask your professor if you can use the PC format -- it will save paper. When you print your return, you will have to confirm your desire to use the PC format by clicking "1040PC Format for Filing" in the Print window.

When you come to the bottom of the worksheet, you will see a box with the notation to **QuickZoom** to the Form 1040. The **QuickZoom** feature is used throughout TurboTax to move from summary schedules and forms to the supporting worksheets and schedules. If there is a supporting form or worksheet for any line on a form, the phrase "Click the attached button to view the supporting field" will appear on the status line, the last row of the screen.

The use of the **QuickZoom** feature is fundamental to the Forms Method. Form 1040 is the general summary form for all tax returns. Once you move to Form 1040, the procedure to follow is to go down Form 1040 line by line. When you come to an income item that applies to you, double click on the small magnifying glass icon, adjacent to the current field, to quick zoom to the supporting forms or worksheets. When you complete the supporting form, close it by clicking on either the "Close" button on the blue title bar or by clicking on the dash in the upper left corner, if you are using Windows 3.1, or the X in the upper right hand corner, if you are using Windows 95. You will close the supporting form and move to the higher level form, returning to Form 1040 when all support forms are closed. Then move to the next applicable line. You continue through Form 1040 until you have completed your tax return.

As you complete the forms and schedules, you will note that TurboTax has added detail boxes, called "smart worksheets," to the forms and schedules for your convenience. The purpose is to give you more guidance and room to include your transactions. These added boxes will not print when you print your return. They are there only for your use.

Three important aids need to be emphasized. One is the Forms Menu. The purpose of this menu is to give you a list of all forms available for completion with this version of TurboTax. If you know which form you need to complete, Schedule C for business income for example, you can move directly to the form by using the Form Selection Menu. You can select the menu by clicking on "Forms" at the top of the screen. Then, click on either the "Open a Form ..." option or the "Show My Return ..." option on the pull-down menu.

Frequently, you will not recall the form to use. The Tools menu option, Search Topics, is designed to help you identify the form you need. The option works like most search options in Windows based software. Selecting the Search Topics option opens a box with two response boxes. In the first, you enter description of the transaction. TurboTax will search the listing of topics and display those that match your request in the second response box. You select the one you want and click on the "Display Topic" button at the bottom of the dialog box. TurboTax takes you to the appropriate EasyStep Interview question for this topic. In entering the description of your problem, try to use general terms. For example, if you ask for information on "poker losses" you will not get the results you desire. But if you use "gambling losses," you will be taken to the exact part of the Interview that relates to gambling losses. What could be easier?

A third aid is similar to the **FastTrack** option in the EasyStep Interview, discussed briefly in Chapter 3. The feature is called, "**Which Forms to Complete**" You select this option by clicking on Forms at the top of the screen. Then select "Open a Form," then select "Which Forms to Complete." (It is near the top of the listing of Form 1040 supporting forms and worksheets.) You will see a listing of the common income and deduction items. You can mark those that apply to your tax return. To the left of each item is a **QuickZoom** button. Click on the button and quick zoom to the appropriate form or worksheet.

When you have completed the worksheet or form, close it and you return to the **Which Forms to Complete** screen.

At any time you can select the EasyStep icon and move to the EasyStep Interview to complete any part of a return. If you have completed the **"Which Forms to Complete**?" worksheet, EasyStep will walk you through the appropriate forms for the items you have selected. If you want to use EasyStep for only one form, you can complete that form with the help of EasyStep and then click on the Go To Forms icon to return to the Forms Method.

DATA ENTRY USING THE FORMS METHOD

The TurboTax screen displays about one-third of the tax form, schedule or worksheet. The display acts as a window through which the form is viewed in the same manner as an electronic spreadsheet works. The user can move up or down the form with the normal movement keys -- the scroll bar at the right of the screen, Up Arrow, Down Arrow, Page Up or Page Down keys.

The specific areas on the tax forms, schedules and worksheets that are designed to receive information are referred to as fields. TurboTax uses a box with white background as a field indicator to highlight the current location of the cursor. The width of the cursor corresponds to the width of the field to which data will be entered. If you enter text data, TurboTax will vary the point size so that the data will fit the space available.

The forms on the screen have six types of fields:

- Text Input Fields
- Numeric Input Fields
- Calculated Value Fields
- Itemized Value Fields
- Overridden Value Fields
- QuickZoom Fields

Each of these fields are discussed below. The type of field will be indicated on the status bar, the last row on the screen, at the right hand corner of that row.

Text Input Fields

Text input fields are the areas into which you enter text information such as names, dates, addresses and descriptions. The current field is highlighted by the box field cursor. If the field is a transferred field, it is "non-enterable." Thus, you will not be able to enter any data in that field. You will see that such fields have a dark-line box around the field and on the left side of the status bar at the bottom of the screen, the phrase "This value is automatically calculated," will be displayed. If you attempt to enter data, TurboTax displays a note suggesting that you click on the attach button to view the supporting data. To overwrite the field, you click on the **right** button and select the "Override" option. It is not a good idea to override fields. If the field is an enterable field, you can reenter data by simply typing in the highlighted field.

Numeric Input Fields

Numeric input fields are the areas into which you enter numbers. If nothing has been entered, the field is blank. If the field is enterable, it will have a field indicator box around it. In the lower left hand corner, the status bar will advise you to "Type in a number." Negative numbers are entered by pressing the minus sign and then the number. Commas are appropriately added by TurboTax when you press the Enter key. To enter cents, you must enter the decimal. Percentages must be entered in their decimal form, thus "10%" is entered ".1." The numbers can be changed by simply entering the correct amount in the same field, thereby replacing the earlier data. TurboTax will "round off" cents to dollars when transferring some data between forms.

Calculated Value Fields

Calculated value fields can be either text or numeric values that are automatically calculated by TurboTax based upon data you have entered. The values are carried forward from other forms or computed from the information on the current form. You can not make entry to these fields except by using the Override feature. Normally you do not wish to do that. The field indicator box for calculated value fields is a thick dark box around the field.

Itemized Value Fields

TurboTax provides the capability to prepare an itemized list of items and total the amounts. The totals are then entered in the numeric field supported by the itemized list. To create an itemized listing simply click on the small itemized statement icon that is adjacent to the field. Clicking the icon will open an itemized statement for your use.

Overridden Value Fields

At times you may make an error in a supporting schedule and want to just correct the total and not bother with correcting the supporting schedule. This is not good. To do so creates bad habits and is an incorrect use of the flexibility in TurboTax. However, there are some occasions where TurboTax does not provide for a rarely used allocation method and you will have to override a calculated value in order to get your desired results. The Override option under the Edit Menu allows you this flexibility. (You can also select

Override by clicking on the right button of the mouse and then select the Override option.) If you do override a field, a note on the status bar (at the bottom of the screen) saying, "You have replaced the value automatically calculated by TurboTax" will appear. With a color monitor, Overridden fields are displayed in Red. Seriously, it is rarely necessary to use the Override feature; do so with caution.

Formatting Data

TurboTax will automatically format data to its common forms. Thus, Social Security or Federal Employer's ID numbers are formatted automatically. Also, for numeric entries over 1,000, TurboTax will insert the appropriate commas. Negative numbers are simply entered with a leading minus sign.

Date fields are used in some forms. **Dates must be entered in the form "mm/dd/yy,"** so that TurboTax can properly compute depreciation deductions and other related calculations. If the month or day is only one digit, you must add a leading zero. Thus, January 1, 1997, must be entered as 01/01/97. While troublesome, it is common to have this restriction.

Checking Boxes

Frequently you will be required to check boxes to indicate your selection. For example, the filing status is indicated by checking the box by the status name. To check the box, simply move the pointer to the box and click once. Clicking a second time will remove the check. If multiple boxes can be checked, simply move to the next one and click. If only one box can be checked, your first check will be removed when you enter the second check. Similarly, if you are required to enter a Yes or No, you can click in the box labeled "Yes." If no box, enter a Y or N.

THE COLOR OF FIELDS

If you have a color monitor, TurboTax displays certain types of fields in different colors as your cursor highlights them. With practice you will be able to recognize the source of the entry by these colors. The two major colors are blue, which indicates data that you have entered, and black, the color used for calculated values.

Color	Type of Entry
Blue	Data entered by you
Black	Data calculated or transferred by TurboTax
Green	Data imported from another program
Magenta	Amount from an itemization
Aqua	Data transferred from last year's file, or from a federal return to a state return
Red	Calculated value overridden by you, or an error
Red *Italicized*	An entry marked as **estimated** by you

USE OF THE KEYBOARD

The mouse is the primary means of operating TurboTax. However, much of the data you enter is done with the keyboard. You will find that the keys are used in a manner similar to many business software products. Below is a listing of the keys and their use in TurboTax.

<ENTER> -- Used to indicate that you have completed entering a field, or that you have selected a command. By default, TurboTax automatically moves the cursor to the next field after you press the enter key. The order of movement is from top to bottom and from left to right.

<TAB> -- As with other Windows software, the TAB key is used to move between options within dialog boxes.

Each of the menu options have speed keys, a combination of the Control key and a letter. These keys can be used in the place of selecting from the menu or icons. For example, Ctrl A will access the Forms Menu. If you use TurboTax for a period of time, you will find these keys very useful. However, most professors will not assign that many problems during a semester; thus, you may not use these speed keys at all.

WORKSHEETS AND FORMS

Inputting tax data follows the flow of paper tax returns. To make it easier to enter certain types of information, TurboTax uses a variety of worksheets. The worksheets are listed in the **Forms** Menu under the form or schedule they support. The entries you make on the worksheets result in entries on the tax forms. You will greatly appreciate these worksheets when you get to the more complicated areas of income taxes, for example passive activities.

A second type of worksheet, referred to as a "Smart Worksheet," appears on some of the forms themselves. These smart worksheets are short and relate to the form currently in use. They will not be printed on the face of the form; they are printed separately. You can hide or show the display of smart worksheets at any time by selecting the appropriate setting in the Options window (under the Edit menu.) However, they are provided to help you. TurboTax strongly encourages you to leave the display of the smart worksheets on, and there is no advantage to not using them. It will be a truly unusual person who elects to turn the smart worksheets off.

TurboTax supports up to ten W-2 forms -- that should cover most part-time jobs. To enter the second or more, simply double click on Line 7 of Form 1040. The screen will display a dialog box that lists all W-2's that have been entered. You will be requested to select one of the listed W-2's or to **create** a new W-2. The same procedure is used for 1099INTs, that report interest income; and K-1's that report income from partnerships, S Corporations, and estates and trusts. The worksheets created appear on the screen in the same format as the paper source document, thus data entry is made easy -- you just fill in the blanks. The individual forms are summarized by TurboTax on summary worksheets and then the totals are transferred to Form 1040 or other appropriate schedule. The system supports all lines on a K-1 form, thus rather complex transactions are made simple -- TurboTax takes the information from the K-1 and puts it on the appropriate form even if it involves passive losses or alternative minimum tax.

PRINTING THE RETURN

The final step is to print the tax return. Before you print the tax return, however, you must inform TurboTax what printer you will be using. By default, TurboTax selects the printer you installed with Windows. If you are still using the same printer, you do not need to set up the printer again. If you change printers, first select **File Print** from the menu, then select the "Setup" button at the bottom of the Printing Dialog Box, as shown in Figure 4-1, below. After selecting the option, select "Specific Printer" bullet to display a window with a list of printers. Use the arrow keys to move up or down the printer list. When your printer appears press the enter key to install TurboTax for your printer. You can change the option at any time by simply repeating the process. If your specific printer is not on the list, select one that is compatible to it. Since TurboTax is using Windows Print Manager to manage the printing, you should always find your printer listed.

The **File Print** and **File Print Setup** commands are very important. These are the commands that are used to put your return on paper. The **Print** command is used to print your tax return. Notice that the default setting is to print the returns from "Front to Back." That is very useful if you are impatient to see the final results. The choice you make will depend on your printer. If output is face up, you need to change the order to Back to Front. Otherwise, the default "Front to Back" is OK. The important point is that you have a choice and that you express that choice every time you print.

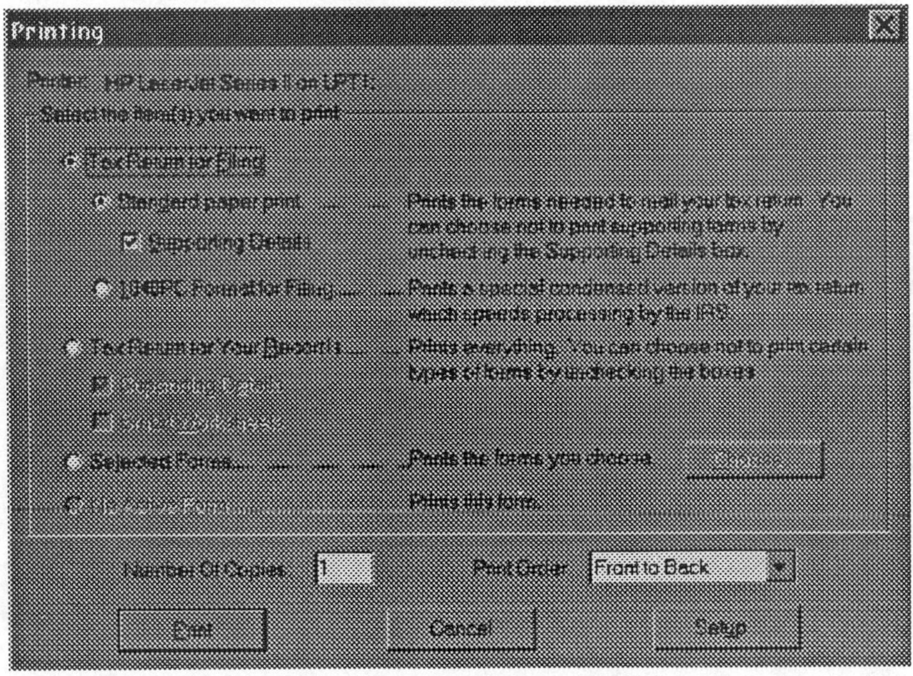

Figure 4-1 Printing Dialog Box

Note that you also have options to print Selected Forms, for example Form 1040, all forms, all worksheets, or all forms and worksheets -- "the whole thing." You can also print multiple copies of your return. You make your selection and click "Print" to continue.

Before you print a return, you should select Final Review to have TurboTax look over your return before you print. Recall that you are printing a graphical format, thus, with a dot matrix printer, the printer prints one dot at a time. It will take some time. Exactly how long depends on your printer. If you select Final Review first, you can save yourself significant hours watching a printer work. That is boring, but it seems irresistible.

Lastly, the first time you attempt to print a form, I suggest that you print only one form, i.e. select the File Print option “Selected Forms” and print any one form. If your printer is not correctly selected, you will know it immediately. Check your printer configuration and try again.

SAVING FILES IN TURBOTAX

You can save as many files in the current directory as you desire. Also you select the filename. TurboTax adds the filetype "TAX," but you can identify the return anyway you desire. I suggest that you use some part of the taxpayer's name. For example when you do Mary Brown's return in Chapter 5, I suggest that you use the name "MBROWN" as your file name. If you are using Windows 95, I suggest you use “Mary_Brown” for the file name. At the time you save the file, you will have to specify the desired directory if you want to save the file in another directory. For example, if you wanted to save MBROWN on a floppy disk in the A drive, you would specify the file name as **A:\MBROWN**. The actual filename will be "MBROWN.TAX" and you will be able to find it when you use the **File Open** option. The file contains only the data; none of the form itself is saved with the data. When you open the file, data is added to the appropriate forms throughout in the program.

TURBOTAX COMMANDS

The Forms Method expects you to interact with the TurboTax commands. Most of the commands are self-explanatory. In fact many of the commands are common to all Windows software. The purpose of this section (albeit a bit long) is to discuss each of the commands available in TurboTax. The commands are discussed in some length; perhaps more than you need. For those of us who do not like to read as much, I suggest that you refer to Figure 4-2. Here you will find a concise listing of the TurboTax commands, any related icon, and a brief statement of what the command does. The discussion that follows is intended to be a reference section, one that you will refer to often, but not necessarily read at one sitting.

Figure 4-2 TurboTax Commands

Menu	Command	Function
File	New Tax Return-Ctrl + N	To begin a new tax return
	Open Tax Return-Ctrl + O	To open an existing tax return, one that has been previously worked on
	Save-Ctrl+S	Saves a tax return data file to disk using same name as current file
	Save As	Saves tax return with a different name
	Go to State	Toggles between state and federal tax return
	Remove State	Erases data for state return
	Transfer	Transfers carryover tax data from prior year TurboTax tax data file
	TaxLink	Creates links between accounting software such as Quicken or QuickBooks and TurboTax
	Import	Copies data from accounting software to TurboTax
	Remove Imported Data	Deletes data from tax return data that has been imported
File	Print-Ctrl + P	Opens the File Print dialog box which allows you to print tax return or selected forms
	Print Setup	Modifies settings for printer
	Electronic Filing	Interfaces with TurboTax electronic filing service
	Exit	Closes TurboTax. Gives opportunity to save a file before closing.
Edit	Undo	Removes last entry
	Cut, Copy, Paste	Common Windows commands to use clipboard for moving data around
	Override - Ctrl + D	Allows user to write over fields whose data are transferred from elsewhere
	Add Supporting Detail-Ctrl+I	Used to add an itemization list to support data entered in a field
	Mark Estimated (F8)	Marks a field as estimated data. Estimates will appear as errors in Review

Edit	Options	Allows user to display or not display Smart worksheets, Tool bar, Error Alerts, and Status bar.
	Sort Table	Sorts a listing of data items
	Delete Table Row	Erases one row of a table
Forms	Go to Forms	Toggles between Forms Method and EasyStep Method
	Open a Form - Ctrl + A	Opens listing of all available forms from which user may select a specific form
	Show My Return - Ctrl + M	Opens a listing of forms that are used with the current tax return
	QuickZoom - Ctrl + Q	Moves from higher level form to supporting form or worksheet
	Remove	Allows user to delete current form
	Link Field	Allows user to link the current field to data from an accounting software such as QuickBooks.
	Select Line - Ctrl + L	Moves to a specified field on the current form
	Forms Errors - Ctrl + E	Displays a list of errors in tax return
	Find Next Error - F7	Moves to next field in current form that has an error in the data for that field
	New Copy, Next Copy, Previous Copy	Moves between multiple worksheets such as W-2 worksheets, K-1 worksheets, etc
	Magnify all forms	Increases or decreases size of data in field
EasyStep	Back to interview	Continues EasyStep interview where you left off when file was saved
	Guide Me	Opens detailed interview for current form, used with Forms Method
	1 - 7 steps	The steps in EasyStep

Tools	My Tax Data	Lists data for current tax return, how it was entered, and where it appears in return
	Final Review	Performs a software check of return
	Search Topics	Opens list of topics and moves you to the correct location in EasyStep for the data
	Calculator	Opens an on-screen calculator - *nice*
	Tax Summary Ctrl + T	Displays current value of key lines of the current tax return
	What-if Worksheet	Used for tax planning. Displays for alternatives for selected tax lines
	History Report	Displays data for a total of five years of returns
Window	Tile, Cascade, Arrange Icons, Close Window, Close All Windows	Same Windows options as are available with all Windows software. Impacts how your screen will appear
Help	Tax Help	TurboTax's tax related topics presented with a search window
	Government instructions	IRS instructions relating to current form
	Data Source	Displays where the data came from
	Program Help	TurboTax's help topics relating to using the software -- have a search window
	What's New This Year?	Reports the changes in both the tax law and in TurboTax effective for the tax year of your tax return.
	Search for Help On	Opens a topic window with selected topics
	WWW Browser Setup	Sets up your TurboTax to access the Internet
	TurboTax Web Site	Enables you to access the TurboTax web site.
	Product updates	Accesses the Intuit/TurboTax web site on the Internet
	Online Registration	Allows you to register your copy of TurboTax with Intuit via the Internet
	Online Support Solutions	Connects you with support found on the TurboTax web site.
	About TurboTax	The people behind the product

The commands help you to use the Forms Method. The focus of the Forms Method is to fill-out the appropriate tax forms. As such, you have to decide what form to use for a given transaction and then follow the instructions on the form to correctly report that transaction. TurboTax helps you in several ways. If there are several steps to completing the form, TurboTax provides a separate worksheet that breaks the form into various parts so that you can enter the data in the simplest way possible. The worksheet summarizes information and records it on the appropriate line on the form. You also have the **TOOLS** command option, **Search Topics**, that helps you find the correct place to report a transaction. When you find your topic, TurboTax moves you from the Forms Method to the EasyStep Method where you are led through the transaction. If you do not want to be led, you can click on the "Go To Forms" button in the lower left hand corner and return to the form.

Figure 4-3 below is a quick reference guide for finding the appropriate TurboTax command to accomplish certain tasks. If the task that you want is not listed here, click on the Tools option and then click on the Search Topics option to access the TurboTax index for its "help" topics.

Task you want to do	Command to use	Page Reference
Change your directory	File Save As, identify directory as part of the filename	Page 4-14
Enter tax data	Enter Key & Arrow keys	Page 4-3
Help using TurboTax	Help	Page 3-5
Help with tax law	Help, Tax help	Page 3-5
Help with tax law, more detailed	Help, IRS Instructions	Page 3-5
Install TurboTax	Install (SETUP.EXE)	Page 2-5
Loading TurboTax	Double Click on Hat	Page 2-12
Moving cursor	Arrow keys, etc	Page 4-6
Printing tax return	File, Print, Tax return for IRS	Page 4-15
Printing all worksheets	File Print, Tax return for your records	Page 4-15
Quitting TurboTax	File, Exit	Page 4-19
Save your tax return	File, Save tax return	Page 4-14
Select a tax form	File, Open Form	Page 4-14
Starting a return	File, New Tax Return	Page 4-14

Figure 4-3 Quick Reference to TurboTax Commands

The focus of TurboTax is on completing a tax return, not on using commands. Accordingly, you will only need to use commands to get help in deciding how to report a transaction, to print the tax return, to save the file, or to setup TurboTax. When you select the Forms Method, TurboTax provides you with the forms; you simply enter your (i.e. your client's) data on the form. You use your mouse to move on the form and between the forms. The worksheets and summary forms have instructions and icons that move you (its called QuickZoom) to supporting forms. TurboTax Help Commands are available should you need to get help either using the program or understanding the tax law -- just click on the ?Help icon.

FILE

The FILE menu contains the commands used in handling data files. The **New Tax Return** option is used to create a new return. When you select this option, the Personal Information Worksheet is displayed. You enter the taxpayer's personal data, i.e. name, address, social security numbers, and other information that is used throughout the return. The **Open Tax Return** option allows you to load an existing file, identified by its filename, from disk storage. The **Save ...** option transfers the data for file specified from RAM to a data disk or directory, i.e., it saves the file, but does not exit the file. A file is closed when you select **New Tax Return**, or when you select **File Exit**. The **Save As ...** command allows you to save the return using another name, perhaps for backup purposes. To save in a different directory, specify the directory as part of the filename, e.g. A:\BillClin.TAX. These commands work in a similar manner in all Microsoft Windows based software.

The **Goto State** moves from the federal tax return module to a state tax return module. You must have the TurboTax software for your state. That software is not included with the South-Western package of TurboTax. At the end of this manual, you will find information about how to obtain the related state software. With this command you can toggle between the state module and the federal module. The software works the same in both modules. Thus, when in the state module, this options reads "Goto Federal." The **Remove State . .** option allows you to erase the existing state return. Perhaps you have made so many data entry errors that it is easier to just erase the whole thing and start over. This option supports that desire.

The **Transfer ...** option transfers files created by last year's edition of TurboTax for Windows to the current version. The result is a newly converted file that contains carry over information from the prior year return, including the taxpayer's name and other identifying information. It is a great time saver. However, since this is the first time most of you have used TurboTax, you will not get to use this option. You will have to type all the data from scratch. Life is tough!

The **TaxLink...** option is designed with the Quicken or QuickBooks user in mind. If you identify the tax related accounts in your Quicken or QuickBooks accounting software, you can electronically copy that data directly to TurboTax. Thus, if you have recent versions of Quicken or Quickbooks, linking your accounting records to TurboTax is very simple.

The **Import...** option is for those who use older versions of Quicken, QuickBooks, or other accounting software and want to import data into TurboTax. Any accounting software that supports the Tax

Exchange Format (TXF) files can also be imported to TurboTax using the **Import** command. The result is the transfer of data from the accounting software to the tax preparation software, TurboTax. This feature, common to many tax preparation software packages, allows data to be transported between tax prep software. The **Remove Imported Data** does just what it says -- it deletes imported data.

FILE PRINT COMMAND

The **File Print** menu is very user friendly, most of the time. The exception is the unlikely case where your printer is not supported by TurboTax. If your printer is supported, the menu will lead you through the process. Using the **Print** menu is intuitive and should provide no problems AFTER you have selected your printer. TurboTax will get the basic printer information from Windows. Thus, in most cases, you just confirm the setup. However, if your printer is not directly supported, try to select one that is similar to your printer. Normally you can find one that will produce acceptable output.

When you click on the **Print** command, you are presented with the Printing dialog box shown in Figure 4-1 above. At the top of the screen the currently selected printer is listed. If this is not the correct printer, i.e. it is not the printer that is currently connected to the PC you are using, you must use the **Printer Setup** option, on the Printing dialog box, to change the selected printer. If you are using this package in a PC lab, check the setup before you print. Things may have changed since you last used the lab. In most college labs, that happens frequently.

The next section prompts you to select the items you want to print. You have four options:

- **Tax Return for Filing** -- If you select this option, the return will be printed with all the schedules and forms required for filing. A suboption, selected by clicking on the adjacent box, will print any itemization statements that were created. These statements provide detailed listings of items that are summed and reported on the various forms and schedules. For most problems, this is the option that you will use.

- **Tax Return for Your Records** -- Use this option to print "the whole thing." In addition to all forms and schedules, you can also print the Itemizations and Smart Worksheets by clicking on the adjacent box. Thus, this option provides you with a paper backup of all of the tax return.

- **Selected Forms** -- If you wish to print only selected forms, schedules, or worksheets, this is the option for you. If you select this option, the box to the right, **Choose...**, will be highlighted and will allow you to specify the form, schedule, or worksheet that you want to print. Thus, if you wish a second copy of a form, a blank copy of a form to share, or perhaps you need only some forms for you state return, the Selected Forms option allows you to print only what you need.

- **Form 1040** or other form, it varies -- The last option prints the current form or schedule. The form named will be the current form, thus if it says Form 1040, only Form 1040, pages 1 and 2, will be printed.

In the area below, you are provided an opportunity to specify the number of copies you need of your return. Also, you can change the print order from Front to Back to Back to Front. Why? If your printer outputs the printed page face up, you should select Back to Front so that your output will be in order when the print job is complete. If face down, select Front to Back and all will be well.

The final section of the Print screen gives the option to **Print**, which will print the return; **Cancel**, which allows you to return to the tax return to do more work; **Setup...**, which moves you to the Printer Setup command where you can modify the printer selected; and **Help** which opens the Program Help window.

PRINT SETUP

With TurboTax for Windows, the basic setup is handled by Windows. However, there is some "fine tuning" that you need to do. The importance of these options varies with the printer that you are using. Recall that printers require special software, called printer drivers, designed just for them. TurboTax assumes that you keep these drivers up-to-date; thus, be certain that you are using the latest driver for your printer. Not much has changed with dot matrix printers in recent years, thus you are probably safe in assuming that you have the current driver for any dot matrix printer.

LaserJet Series and Compatible

In general, when using HP's LaserJet printers, you should select Portrait orientation, 8.5 by 11 inch or letter size paper, and set the resolution to 300 dpi. No special font cartridges are needed; TurboTax provides its own "soft fonts." Always select "None" in the Cartridge Selection List on the Printer Setup window. If you have problems printing with your laser printer, try selecting the HP III LaserJet printer. Most laser printers will work well with the drivers for this basic laser printer. If problems continue, check your printer driver. If it is HPPCL5A.DRV, the driver that originally was shipped with Windows 3.1, update the driver to HPPCL5MS.DRV which is included on your TurboTax disk and by default it is in the TAX95 directory (or folder.) If you are using HP Laser Jet 4 or compatible, use **Print Setup** to set the resolution to 300 dpi.

9-pin and 24-pin Print Setup

If your printer has a quality option, select NLQ (Near Letter Quality). For a 9-pin printer, select 120x144 graphics resolution. If you have a 24-pin printer, select the middle resolution, e.g., for the Epson LQ series, select 180x180 resolution.

HP DeskJet and DeskJet Plus

TurboTax does not directly support the use of the DeskJet printers due to limitations in the printer's use of soft fonts. However, these printers can be used successfully with SuperPrint Jr. software or when used with the Epson F-80 emulation cartridge for 9-pin dot matrix printing.

To use the Epson F-80 emulation properly, you must install the Epson F-80 printer driver (a 9-pin driver) into Windows. This can be done through the Windows Printer Control Panel in the Main Program Group. Consult you Windows User's Guide for details.

If your printer has a quality option, select NLQ (Near Letter Quality). Also, select 120x72 graphics resolution.

PREVENTING PRINTING TRUNCATION

With some printers, some forms will truncate, or cut-off, the very bottom of the forms. The problem is that the default margins of these printers are slightly larger than the forms require. In most cases no crucial data is lost, but the form may not look its best. Perhaps your professor will not be concerned if the last line is missing. If she/he is concerned, the solution to the missing lines varies with the printer being used. Read on.

Preventing Truncation During Printing

Some forms may be truncated at the bottom when printed on 9-pin and 24-pin printers. This is because the default margin on some printers are slightly different than the forms require. If you experience this problem, follow the instructions below. To discover that you have a problem, print the Form 1040 only, one of the print options. If you will have a problem, you will have it printing this return.

To correct the problem, follow these steps.

1. Select **Print** from the File Menu, and then click on the Setup button in the dialog box.
2. When the Setup window appears, click the **Paper Size** window and change the setting to **User Defined Size**. When the **User Defined Size** dialog box appears, be sure the **Units** are 0.01 inch. In addition, the **Width** must be 850 and the **Length**, 1100.
3. If you are offered a **Margin** button, click on it and select 0 from the Select Margin size box on the right. Repeat this process for the other three settings until they all read = 0 in. (Whether or not you have a margin option depends upon the driver file for your printer.)
4. Click **OK** and proceed with your printing.

IRS PRINTING REQUIRMENTS

The IRS has adapted its printing requirements to recognize the use of personal computers by a large number of people. The requirements are listed for your information.

1. Print the return with black ink on white or cream colored paper, at least 18 pound weight, size 8" x 11" or 8.5"x11". All forms must have a high standard of legibility. Lower quality printers should not be used for the preparation of tax returns. Furthermore, a clean fresh ribbon should be used to insure a dark print.

2. Adjust the page setup to provide a minimum .25" margin on all four sides of the page. Original computer generated forms should be filed, not copies. Vertical spacing should be 6 lines to the inch and horizontal spacing should be 10 characters per inch. All text and numeric data fields must have printer generated underlining.

3. Remove the perforated pin-feed strips on the sides of the paper.

4. Returns must be filed with the forms, schedules and supporting statements assembled in a particular order. Form 1040 always comes first, followed by the forms arranged in order according to the IRS attachment sequence number which is printed in the upper right corner of each form following the year (e.g. "1997 * 08" appears in the upper right corner of the Schedule B). If you need or wish to submit supporting statements with your return, place them behind the required forms and schedules, and arrange them in the same order as the forms and schedules that they support.

5. You are not required to submit itemization details other than what is asked for on the official forms and schedules. If you do wish to submit any of them, arrange them (and any other supporting statements you are filing) in the same order as the forms and schedules they support.

6. Both spouses, if applicable, must sign the copy of the Form 1040 that you submit to the IRS. **Do not submit a return with a photocopied signature.**

7. Use the IRS preprinted mailing label and envelope, if possible.

ELECTRONIC FILING

Prepares your tax return for electronic filling. Since you will be filing the old fashioned way, on paper to your professor, you will not need this command.

LISTED FILES

The files listed above the Exit option are the most recent files that you accessed with TurboTax. Thus, if you start one problem, close it and start a second, then go back to the first, you can look at this list of files and open the first directly from the list. This makes life simpler.

FILE EDIT

Exit allows the user to exit TurboTax and return to the Program Manager or the Desktop with Windows 95. If you have made changes to the return which have not been saved, you will be prompted to save these before you exit.

EDIT COMMAND

The **Edit** commands allow you to change entries. The first option **Undo** reverses your last command or keystroke thereby allowing you to change the contents of a single field. If you entered an error, you can Undo and return to the point just before you pressed the enter key or click the mouse. If you have not yet entered the data, the option is not available.

You also have the standard editing commands available with all Windows software. Thus, you can **Cut**, **Copy**, or **Paste** one field to another.

You have the option to **Override** a field that is calculated or transferred from elsewhere. If the field cannot be overridden, the option will appear gray and will display **Can't Override**. It is not a good idea to override. As you can't fool Mother Nature, TurboTax will rarely treat a transaction in such a way that you will have to override. If you are not careful which field you override, the overridden data can not transfer to other forms correctly. You certainly will have more work to do to check the return if you elect to override. Thus, I urge you to not do it.

The **Add Supporting Details** option opens an itemization window that lets you enter descriptions and amounts for up to 30 items that will be totaled and put on a single entry line. You can also select the **Supporting Details** icon or button adjacent to the current field to select or create an itemization schedule for that field. These are very useful when you have a long list of items to enter, for example a list of medical expenses. Note that the Itemization will also do the arithmetic and total the itemized amounts. You can also use these statements to add notes and other supporting statements.

The **Mark Estimated** option allows you to mark a field as an estimated amount. Thus, you can compute an estimated tax before you have the final numbers. The field that is marked as estimated will be displayed in italic. Also, when you select the **Forms errors** option, selected by clicking on the yellow triangle with an exclamation point and the words "Forms Errors" icon, the errors listed will include any fields that are estimated. By highlighting the estimated field and double clicking, TurboTax will move you to the estimated field so you can enter the final information. When you move to an estimated field, the option is changed to **Unmark Estimated**. Thus, when you have all the information, you can move to the estimated field using the **Forms Errors** option, enter the final information, and then unmark the field with the **Edit Unmark Estimated** option.

The **Options** feature allows you limited control over the appearance of the screen. The default is to display all of the features. I suggest that you stay with the default. The features that can be changed are to show or not to show **Smart Worksheets**, the **Tool Bar**, **Error Alerts**, and **Status Bar**.

The last two options support the editing of tables -- for example a listing of dividends received. The **Sort Table** option allows you to sort, in alphabetic order for example, a table. The **Delete Table Row** deletes a row in a table. After deleting rows, you can use the **Sort Table** option to close the gap. Enough said.

FORMS MENU

The Forms Method is built around your use of forms. You select the form that you need to fill out and do it. The **Forms Menu** brings together the commands that support your use of forms. The first option, "Go To Forms," is active only when you are using EasyStep. It serves the same purpose as the "Go To Forms" icon at the bottom of the EasyStep window, that is you move to the forms. The next option, **Open a Form**, can be used to access any of the forms available with TurboTax. You can select it from the menu or by using the Forms icon on the Tool Bar. Click on the icon or select the menu option and a listing of the available forms is displayed in a pull-down menu with a scroll bar on the right. Scroll down the listing until you come to the form you need. Double click on the form name and you will move to the form ready to enter the appropriate data.

The option, **Show my Return**, displays the forms on which you have entered data or to which data has been transferred. If you need to move to a form that you have used previously, the listing displayed by **Show my Return** will be shorter and provide a faster access to the desired form than that provided by the first option. Unfortunately, there is no icon to support this command. But, when you click on the Open a Forms icon, the forms window provides you the option to switch between **Open a Form** and **Show my Return**. Thus, you are only two clicks away from seeing your forms list.

QuickZoom is a great help in getting around the forms. The command lets you move to a specific form that is attached or linked to the current field. By using the Form 1040 as "command center" and using **QuickZoom** to move between Form 1040 and the supporting forms, you can efficiently move through a tax return. For example, move the cursor to Line 7 on Form 1040 and double click. TurboTax will take you to the W-2 Worksheet module where you enter the data from your Form W-2, relating to salaries and wages. TurboTax picks up the data from the W-2 Worksheet and places it on the appropriate forms. If you have multiple W-2s, simply click on Line 7 again and you will be able to create a new W-2 Worksheet to create your second W-2 . If there is a supporting form for a line on a form, QuickZoom will be active in the Forms Menu. Also, the magnifying glass icon will be attached to the field.

The option **Remove <form>** is available to delete the current form from your return. Actually, the form itself is a part of TurboTax and will always be available, but this option will delete any data you have entered, and remove the current form from your return. Be careful when you delete a form. If any data is transferred from that form to another, you will be changing the second form also. Normally, this is good. However, just be aware.

Link Field allows you in special circumstances to designate a form to which the amount should be transferred. These circumstances occur when an amount can appear on more than one form. The occurrence of these multiple possibilities for transferring amounts is rare, so do not expect to use this command often. One example is when you sell depreciable assets; you may have to link a field to Form 6252. Frequently, TurboTax will use this option without your selecting it. It is very user friendly in that regard.

The **Select Line** option allows you to specify a specific line on the current form and move directly to that line. It can be useful in moving around a tax return.

The **Form Errors** option displays a listing of fields that contain errors or are marked as estimates. The command is supported with a button, a small yellow triangle with an exclamation point in its center icon, and the words "Form Errors." You can select any field from the list, move to that form, and correct the error. Some of the errors have no impact on the computation of the tax and are there to provide information used by the IRS or on the state tax return. Thus, an error is frequently the omission of information. This is a command we all need; well maybe not you and I, but all those other people who make errors. Actually, TurboTax keeps track of errors it detects as you go along. When you run the **EasyStep** option **Review**, TurboTax uses the **Form Errors** command to organize these errors, and then moves you to each, one at a time.

The errors are stored continuously as you complete the return, thus, you can go to any form and elect the **Find Next Error** command (or press F7, Function Key 7,) to move to the line on the form that contains an error. Press F7 a second time and you will move to the next error. When you can move no farther, you have reached the last error on that form. Then move to the next form and repeat the process to correct the errors without directly using the **Review** feature.

The **New, Next, and Previous Copy** command helps you to move among the various information forms you receive, such as W-2s, 1099's, etc. The **New Copy** allows you to create a new form. The **Magnify Form** command is similar to the ZOOM command in most Windows software. The command will enlarge the screen and make the data easier to read. The default is 100 percent; keep it.

EASYSTEP MENU

The **EasyStep Menu** connects the Forms Method and the EasyStep approach. You can use this menu option to move to the EasyStep approach at any one of the seven steps. Thus, you are able to use the convenience of **EasyStep** to help you complete a particularly difficult form and then return to the Forms Method to complete the remainder of the return. To return to the Form, click on the *GoTo Forms* icon in the lower right corner of the **EasyStep** screen. Refer to Chapter 3 for a more in depth look at the EasyStep Interview.

The **Go to EasyStep** option will move you from the Forms Method to where you left off in the **EasyStep Method**. This command is supported with an icon, two footprints moving forward and the word "EasyStep". When you come to a difficult area of a tax return, you can select **EasyStep**. In **EasyStep** you can click on the "Where Am I?" tab to list all the steps in the Interview. Then you can move to the specific transaction you are currently struggling with. For example, if you are having trouble deciding how to handle a distribution from an IRA, you could enter **EasyStep**, click on Where Am I? tab, scroll to **Retirement**, and then select **Pension/IRA Distributions**. **EasyStep** will walk you through reporting the IRA distribution. Then, you can return to the forms by clicking on the *GoTo Forms* icon in the lower right corner of the **EasyStep** screen.

Interview uses a dialog box to display its questions and give space for your answers. You supply the information which is then transferred to the appropriate areas of the actual return that is shown in the bottom window on the screen. Normally, you do not enter information **directly** onto the forms while using the Interview. The program does it for you. As you progress through the questions, these forms are automatically updated. A check is placed next to each sub-topic in the list of items after it has been completed. You have the option of clicking on the "Where Am I?" tab and moving to a lower topic, thereby skipping topics that you know are not relevant to the tax return you are completing. Of course if you are not certain of the topics that apply to your return, you should go through all questions to insure that you do not skip an important topic.

If you have selected the "View Current Form" tab, a portion of the current form will be displayed in the bottom half of the screen. While you normally do not enter data directly on the form, you do have the option of making changes directly on the form. Thus, the form is live in the sense that you can edit it. I urge you to only edit the form and not stay in EasyStep and enter data on forms. Use the Forms Method if that is your preferred method. If the data in the field is transferred from another form or worksheet, you will not be able to make changes on that field. You will have to make the changes at the source.

As you move through the Interview, you will notice some of the words in the questions are light blue (on a color monitor) or underlined (on a monochrome monitor). you can move your mouse pointer to these words and click on the words to open TurboTax's on-screen Help to view a definition or explanation of the tax term.

A last EasyStep option, **State Assistant**, is only active when you are using TurboTax state software. Since state software is not available from South-Western, you probably will not see this feature active.

Having the ability of moving between the user friendly **EasyStep** and the efficient Forms Method allows the user to have the best of both worlds. Do not hesitate to use these features. They are in the program to help you complete the return.

TOOLS MENU

The Tools Menu collects the various commands that provide you with convenient tools to help you complete your tax return. The first, **My Tax Data** opens a window listing all of your entries and their respective tax forms and lines. It is a listing of all the information that you entered in completing the tax return. You can move the cursor to any line and double click to move to the highlighted form and line. Once there, you can edit the line and correct any error. Thus, if you misspelled the abbreviation for Virginia, you can scan the "What you entered" column, highlight the error, select "Go to Form," and make your correction.

The **Final Review** option opens the **Review** step of **EasyStep** and performs a review of your tax return. The option will find the errors and then lead you to each one with an opportunity to correct each error.

The **Search Topics** option helps you find where to report those unusual items of income and expense that occur in most tax returns. **Search Topics** works like most search options in Windows based software. Selecting the **Search Topics** option opens a box with two response boxes. In the first, you enter description of the transaction. TurboTax will search the listing of topics and display those that match your request in the second response box. You select the one you want and click on the "Display Topic" button at the bottom of the dialog box. TurboTax takes you to the appropriate EasyStep Interview question for this topic.

The **Calculator** option is very useful. This command opens an on-the-screen calculator with the basic arithmetical functions. In addition, the calculator has a "paste" feature that will put the total shown on the calculator in the current empty field. Data entry is always better if it can be done by the computer.

The **Tax Summary** tool will display on the screen a brief summary of your tax return. It lists the major items such as the total gross income, adjusted gross income, taxable income, taxes, tax withheld and tax due or refund due. You can select the option before and after entering a transaction to see the marginal impact of one specific transaction.

The **What-if Worksheet** allows you to compare the current tax return with three alternatives. The worksheet supports copying the current tax return to the other columns. Then you can make changes to the columns by scrolling to the cell and editing the entry. Thus, you can compare a total of four alternatives at one time. Very useful when you do basic tax planning.

The **History Worksheet** is useful if you have the data. To have the history worksheet automatically created, you must have used TurboTax in the previous year and have a carryover data file that is created when you import your return to the current year. The worksheet reports a total of five years of taxes, the three previous years, the current year and the next year. If this is the first year you have used TurboTax, you can enter the data in each cell by referring to your prior years returns. A five-year summary of your tax returns is very useful in tax planning.

The **Tax Graphs** option will display the current year's tax summary in four graphs. One of the graphs shows you how the Federal government spent your tax dollars.

WINDOW MENU

The **Window Menu** offers three methods of viewing open windows, allows you to quickly close all open windows, and lists each active form and window. These options are common to all Windows software.

Tile arranges all open windows in smaller sizes to fit next to each other on the desktop.

Cascade causes all open windows to overlap so that each title bar is visible. This is the default display. You can of course override this by clicking the right most arrow head on an active form to display the form on the entire screen.

Arrange Icons rearranges the form icons in the bottom left area of your screen so that they are evenly spaced and do not overlap.

Close Windows closes the current window without affecting any other opened windows. The **Close All Windows** closes all the opened windows but does not close TurboTax. To leave TurboTax, you must use the **File Exit** command.

The bottom portion of the Window Menu lists the windows that are currently open in TurboTax. Selecting a window from this list (by double clicking) lets you switch between windows. Thus, you can move between the open windows very easily using this option.

HELP MENU

The Help menu allows you to select from the various sources of help available with TurboTax. The help provided is of two types:

help in using the program and
help understanding the tax law.

The second group of commands can be referred to as "tax aids." Tax aids help screens, display windows, or dialog boxes, give you information about how a transaction is taxed, and what information is required by the IRS. These aids are "dynamic," that is, the available aid changes as you change location in the tax return. Thus, the help given is always relevant to where you are in the forms. These aids will be very beneficial as you begin to prepare tax returns. Recall that one goal of tax education is to train you to know where to find the answer to tax questions and to understand the impact of your answer on the final tax liability. Learning to use the dynamic help available in TurboTax achieves that goal. In using **Help** you will note some words are displayed in light blue or underlined. These words are referred to as "Hypered words" and are linked directly to the relevant text in **Help** that explains the term. To get more information about these terms, click on the word or point to it and press enter.

Three types of help are available: Tax help, Program Help, and Government or IRS Instructions.

Tax Help contains detailed information to help you prepare your return. The option is context sensitive and takes you directly to the topic that applies to the current field. In a general sense, **Tax Help** will tell you how to report the transaction using TurboTax. Also, if you have to enter specialized data, **Tax Help** will give you a list to chose from. For example, if you are self-employed and complete Schedule C, you will have to identify the **SIC** number for your business. **Tax Help** provides you with a listing of all SIC numbers.

Government (IRS) Instructions displays the information in the official printed IRS instructions for the line your cursor is on at the moment you request help. In general, the IRS instructions contain information about the tax law itself. For example, what is required if a taxpayer dies during the tax year is explained in the IRS Instructions.

Program Help provides information about the use of the TurboTax itself. It is context sensitive, thus the help offered is dependent upon where you are in the program at the time you request the help. A typical response will give you a list of questions from which you make your selection to receive the help you need. If your answer is not listed, click on the *Search* button. An indexed listing of terms will be available. You enter the term that describes the help you need and if the term is in the listing, you will move to the **Help** that relates to the term. If your term is not in the list, try a more general term. You also have the option to browse the list of terms to search for the help you need.

What's New This Year? explains the changes in both the tax laws and in TurboTax itself. You can read this and get an idea of the volume and type of changes that tax preparers are faced with each year.

The option, **Search for Help On**, allows you to enter the search module directly from the menu. It works the same as the *Search* button on the general help screen.

World Wide Web is the menu option that will connect you to the TurboTax home page. To use this option, you must have installed the Intuit edition of Netscape. If you have access to a full version of Netscape, which most universities do have, you should not install this restricted version. This means that you will have to save your file, exit TurboTax, load your Netscape and then go to the TurboTax home page using its URL. The Intuit and TurboTax URLs are:

http://www.intuit.com   and   http://www.turbotax.com

There is a wealth of information on this home page. I urge you all to get connected and surf your way to the TurboTax home page. While you are there, check out the Quicken Financial Network home page. It has a lot of information about financial planning, something we all need to do more of.

About TurboTax displays information about the version you are using and about Intuit, the people who develop the software.

TURBOTAX ICONS FOR FORMS METHOD

The **Tool Bar** displayed across the top of the screen lists the most commonly used commands (e.g., File, Edit, etc.). Below the Tool Bar are seven icons and buttons that are <u>only</u> displayed when the Forms Method is selected. Each is discussed briefly.

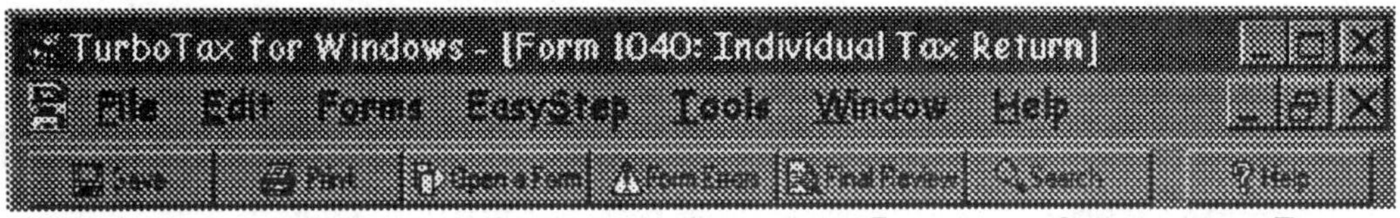

1 2 3 4 5 6 7

1. The first icon is the image of a floppy disk and the word "Save." Clicking the icon will save the current file to the current disk -- **File Save** is the command being used.

2. The second icon is a printer. It is used to print forms from your current tax return.

3. The next icon is the Forms icon, three small forms and the words "**Open a Form**." It displays the Form Selection Menu that lists all available forms, schedules, or worksheets. You will use this option to select the required form. When you enter the Form Selection Menu, you will have the option of listing all forms, or only those that relate to the current tax return. The command being used is the **Forms** command, **Open a Form** option.

4. The fourth icon is a small yellow triangle with an exclamation point in the middle and the words "Form Errors." This icon will display a listing of errors identified by the Final Review feature of TurboTax. You can scroll through the listing and move to the one you are ready to correct. The command used is the **Forms** command, **Form Errors** option.

5. The fifth icon is "**Final Review**." This button will execute TurboTax's review of the tax return and identify those errors listed by the Form Errors icon. The command used is the **Tools** command, **Final Review** option.

6. The next icon is the **Search** button. This button activates the **Tools** command, **Search Topics** option. The command allows you to search from an indexed listing of common tax transactions and receive more information as to the proper treatment of that transaction.

7. The last icon is **?Help**, the icon that activates TurboTax's Help menu. There you will have your choice of three types of help: Tax Help, Government (IRS) Instructions, and Program Help. The help given is for the current field; that is referred to as "context sensitive." The help in TurboTax is useful; expect to use it.

This completes the list of icons on the Tool Bar. You will save time clicking on the icon rather than going to the command menus and selecting the commands. But both ways will get the job done. And that is the important point.

TURBOTAX WORKSHEETS

TurboTax builds the tax return from a foundation of Forms and Schedules that are official IRS documents. To these, TurboTax adds a variety of worksheets designed to facilitate the entry of tax data. Included are "smart worksheets" which are imposed on some of the IRS's forms to aid data entry for that form, and interactive worksheets designed to support complicated transactions, such as the depreciation worksheet -- called the Asset Entry Worksheet. Figure 4-4 lists some of the worksheets used by TurboTax. The worksheets are designed to focus on key information required to correctly report complicated tax transactions. If you do not complete the worksheet, you will have to use the Override command to enter the correct tax data. It easier to use the worksheets. In addition, you might learn some tax law by using the worksheet.

Figure 4-4 TurboTax Worksheets

Form 1040	Personal Information Worksheet, Which Forms to complete, Form W-2: Wage & Tax Statement, Form 1099-Misc Worksheet, Form 1099-R: Pension Distributions, Line 7 Statement, State Tax Refund Worksheet, IRA, Keogh, SEP Contribution Worksheet, Social Security Income Worksheet, Other Income Worksheet, Tax Payments Worksheet, Additional Dependents Statement
Schedule A	Medical Expenses Worksheet, Tax & Interest Deduction Statement, Charitable Contributions Statement, Miscellaneous Itemized Deductions Statement, Itemized Deductions Worksheet
Schedule B	Interest Income Statement, Additional Interest Income Statement, Dividend Income Statement, Additional Dividend Income Statement, Seller-Financed Mortgage Interest Statement.
Schedule D	Additional Capital Gains & Losses Statement, Worksheets for Schedule D
Schedule E	Schedule K-1 Worksheet--Partnership, Schedule K-1 Worksheet--S Corporations, Schedule K-1 Worksheet--Estates & Trusts, Sch E Partnerships & S Corps Report, Sch E:
Schedule EIC	Earned Income Credit Worksheet, Earned Income Worksheet
Schedule R	Sch R AMT Limit Worksheet
Form 4562	Sec 179 Expense Report
Form 8582	Modified AGI Worksheet, Passive Activities Worksheet 1, Passive Activities Worksheet 2, Passive Activities Worksheet 3,4,5,6,Passive Activities Worksheet 1-AMT, Passive Activities Worksheet 2-AMT, 3-AMT,4-AMT,5-AMT,6-AMT
1994 Federal Income Tax Carryover Worksheet	

Smart Worksheets

TurboTax has created *Smart Worksheets* to aid you in entering data. Rather than using a separate worksheet to help you determine the appropriate total, you can use the shorter smart worksheets that are embedded in the form. These worksheets will appear on the screen but will not be printed when the form itself is printed. They are not a part of the official IRS form, rather simply an added space to report the information required by the form. While you can turn off the display of the Smart Worksheets using the **Edit Options** command, I urge you not to do so. The smart worksheets are there for your convenience. Use them.

Data Entry Worksheets

Several of the worksheets are full page worksheets that are designed to aid you in entering data. To use these worksheets enter the detailed tax data as prompted by the worksheet. Then TurboTax takes over and the individual items are totaled, and the totals are transferred by TurboTax to the appropriate line and form. For example, many taxpayers have income from wages or salaries and receive a Form W-2 from their employer. TurboTax has provided a worksheet, called the "Form W-2 Wage & Tax Statement," to summarize W-2 forms.

TurboTax for Windows allows ten W-2's, or "copies" of W-2's per taxpayer. The worksheet mirrors the actual form W-2 received by the taxpayer, thus, the required data can be entered exactly as seen on the W-2. Double clicking on Line 7 of the Form 1040, takes you to the Form W-2 Worksheet. The first step in using the W-2 Worksheet is to enter the employer's name. When you arrive at the W-2 Worksheet, you should note the box at the top of the worksheet that is used to identify the W-2 as for the Spouse or not. The spouse could be either the Husband or the Wife, as long as you are consistent. The W-2 Worksheet asks for the "Control Number." The number is required for electronic filing. Also it is on the W-2, so it is on the worksheet. It has no impact on your tax liability, thus you can skip it if you desire or if the information is not available (as is the case in most of the problems in this manual.) After you have entered all the information from the W-2's, TurboTax will summarize all W-2's and transfer the totals to Line 7 on Form 1040. While you can use the Override command and enter the W-2 amounts directly on Line 7 and other applicable lines, you will find it easier to use the W-2 Worksheet.

The most common way of moving to supporting worksheets or forms is to double click (*QuickZoom*) on the line supported. In addition, you can select the worksheet or form from **Open a Form**. You can access this menu by clicking on the Forms icon on the Tool Bar. If you use the EasyStep approach, TurboTax will select the appropriate worksheet and ask the correct questions, prompting you to enter the required data.

Asset Entry Worksheet

The Asset Entry Worksheet is used to calculate deductions for assets used in a trade or business or held for production of income. This is a very important worksheet and should be used for **ALL** depreciation calculations. The worksheet is very flexible and complete. It will handle substantially all problems with computing depreciation. I urge you to rely on the worksheet. A copy of the worksheet follows on the next two pages. Note that there is a special worksheet for computing depreciation on cars and trucks. It should be used for all computations relating to the use of cars or trucks in a business.

In TurboTax all depreciation related entries (other than those for cars and trucks) are made in the Asset Entry Worksheet. As with all forms in TurboTax for Windows, when you use the Forms Method you start with the field where the final number is reported and *QuickZoom* to the supporting worksheet. Thus, you start by moving the pointer to the field where the depreciation expense is reported, for example Line 13 on Schedule C. Then you QuickZoom (double click) to access the Asset Entry Worksheet. While the IRS uses Form 4562 to report all depreciation expenses, TurboTax takes care of that by transferring the amounts from the worksheet to the appropriate forms. The only place you need to make an entry is on the Asset Entry Worksheet or its first cousin, the Car and Truck Expenses Worksheet which is used for all vehicles.

The Asset Entry Worksheet leads you through the relevant factors that determine the method and amount of depreciation for the various types of assets. The Asset Entry Worksheet makes assumptions based upon your answers. Thus, you may need only answer a few of the questions before TurboTax is able to determine the amount of depreciation for your asset. After you have entered the information in the General Asset Information and Type of Asset sections of the worksheet, frequently the remainder of the worksheet will be automatically computed. Of course you should check page 2 of the worksheet to be certain it is completed. Take a moment to look at the Asset Entry Worksheet on the following pages; it will help you understand the procedure.

The first few times you use the worksheet you need to read carefully. The Asset Entry Worksheet is also used to report the disposition of assets and it includes questions relating to such dispositions. When you record an asset that is purchased in the current year, these questions do not apply. Just ignore them and all will be fine.

If the terms on the Asset Entry Worksheet are not familiar to you, I suggest that you review the Tax Help to investigate the meaning of the terms. Simply move the cursor to the field you have a question about and click on the *Help* icon. Also, I will remind you that you have a textbook that explains how the tax system determines depreciation or cost recovery allowances. It is also useful to you.

Asset Entry Worksheet 1997

Name(s) Shown on Return	Social Security Number
Larry & Pat Graham	234-87-5643

Activity: Sch C Stockbroker

Asset Information (For vehicles, use the Car and Truck Expenses Worksheet)

1	Description of asset	computers	Example: Laser printer
2	Date placed in service	06/15/97	Example: 06/15/97
3	Enter the total cost when asset was acquired	3,500.	Include land for asset type I, J or M
4	Type of asset	A - Computer	
5	Percentage of business use	100.00 %	Range: 1.00 to 100.00 If blank, 100.00% is used
6	Enter the amount of Sec 179 expense elected	0.	Applicable for asset type A thru G. Subject to limitation. See TaxHelp.
7	Total amount of land included in the cost	0.	Applicable for asset type I, J or M
8	Prior depreciation	0.	If blank, prior depreciation from Asset Life History is used. Required if asset was sold.
9	**Depreciation deduction** ►	700.	
10	AMT prior depreciation	0.	If blank, prior depreciation from Asset Life History is used. Required if asset was sold.
11	AMT depreciation deduction	525.	
12	AMT adjustment/preference	175.	See TaxHelp for computation
13	**QuickZoom** to Asset Life History ►		

14 If a computer or peripheral equipment (asset type A), was asset used exclusively at your regular business establishment? ☐ Yes ☒ No

15 If video, photo, or phono equipment (asset type B), was asset used exclusively at your regular business establishment, or in connection with your principal trade or business? ☐ Yes ☐ No

16 Enter the IRC section under which you amortize the cost of intangibles (asset type L) ______

17 Home Office copy number for home office (asset type M) or home office improvement (asset type N) ______

Dispositions — Complete this part only if you sold, abandoned, or otherwise disposed of this asset in 1997. Enter business portion only for all amounts.

18 Date sold, given away, or abandoned in 1997 .... ____________ Example: 12/01/97

19 Sales price .... ____________

20 Expense of sale .... ____________

21 Property type .... ____________

22 If Section 1250:
a Additional depreciation after 1975 .... ____________
b Applicable percentage .... ____________ %
c Additional depreciation after 1969 and before 1976 .... ____________

23 Double click to link sale to Form 6252 .... ► ____________

24 Gain or loss .... ____________

25 AMT gain or loss .... ____________

26 Part of Form 4797 to which gain/loss carries .... ____________

Detail Asset Information — This section is calculated for most assets from the data above.
Use Find Next Error feature to check for any required entries.

		Yes		No	
27	Listed property?	X			See TaxHelp
28	Subject to automobile limitations?			X	
29	Eligible Section 179 property?	X			Applies to current year assets only.
30	Use IRS tables for MACRS property?			X	

Regular Depreciation

31	Depreciation Type	MACRS	
32	Asset class	5	
33	Depreciation Method	200DB	
34	MACRS convention	HY	
35	**QuickZoom** to set 1997 convention ►		
36	Recovery period	5.0	
37	Year of depreciation	1	
38	Depreciable basis	3,500.	See TaxHelp for computation

Alternative Minimum Tax Depreciation

39	AMT basis, if different from cost	
40	If placed in service before 1987, is asset	
41	AMT depreciation method	150DB
42	AMT recovery period	5.0
43	AMT depreciable basis	3,500.

NOTE ABOUT SECTION 179

Section 179 allows taxpayers to expense up to $18,000 (in 1997, more in later years) of tangible personal property used in a trade or business. If the taxpayer is engaged in more than one trade or business (i.e. the taxpayer has more than one Schedule C), each Schedule C must be supported by a different Form 4562. However, TurboTax will transfer ALL SECTION 179 amounts from either the Asset Entry Worksheet or the Car and Truck Expenses Worksheet to the Section 179 Expense Report. From there the amounts are summarized and transferred to Form 4562 if you have only one activity or to Form 4562: Section 179 Limitation, if you have more than one activity. This is the Form 4562 used to report the total Section 179 deduction. If all of your Section 179 deduction applies to one activity, a regular Form 4562 will report all information relating to depreciation and Section 179 expense on the same Form 4562. If you have more than one activity that incurs Section 179 expenses, the limit is determined on Form 4562: Section 179 Limitation and then you have to allocate the total Section 179 allowable deduction to the various Forms 4562. To do so you will have to **Override** the amount on Line 12 of the various Forms 4562 and enter the allocated amount. Of course the total Section 179 expense reported on the various lines 12 can not exceed the total allowable as determined on Form 4562: Section 179 Limitation. This form (Form 4562: Section 179 Limitation) is not printed as a part of the tax return.

A second limit of Section 179 is the taxable income from all trades or businesses. TurboTax computes this amount and enters the total business income on the taxable income limit line, Line 11 of Form 4562. In addition, the overall limit of $18,000 is reduced by the purchase of qualifying assets in excess of $200,000, based upon the total of all transactions incurred by the taxpayer during the year. TurboTax applies the limit on Form 4562, not on the Asset Entry Worksheet. Thus, when you complete the worksheet, the amount of Section 179 deduction may exceed $18,000. When you view Form 4562, you will note that the limit has been applied. Write your Congressman or Senator to try to get this simplified.

In summary, the **Asset Entry Worksheet** is flexible and thorough. I strongly urge you to use it in all cases where the taxpayer has depreciation expenses. The worksheet is flexible enough to correctly compute depreciation for the current year even if you placed the asset in service in an earlier year. The codes used to identify the correct method are complicated, but if you use the worksheet from the start, TurboTax will enter the correct codes for you. That way, it is simple.

INCOME FROM PARTNERSHIPS and S CORPORATIONS

Certain legal entities do not pay income tax directly. These entities pass their income and deductions to their owners and the owners pay the tax. These entities are referred to as "flowthrough entities." Trusts, Estates, Partnerships and S Corporations are the common examples of flowthrough entities. The owners receive a copy of a Schedule K-1 that reports their share of the income, expenses and other tax items from the flowthrough entity.

TurboTax treats the Schedules K-1 in the same manner that Forms W-2 are handled. Thus, the various K-1s (limit of ten) are summarized and reported on the appropriate form. Since the K-1s the taxpayer receives will be substantially identical to the Schedule K-1 worksheets, it is a simple task to enter the amounts in the appropriate places. You need to pay particular attention to the General Information and Activity Information sections at the top of the worksheet. It is here that you will identify if the partnership interest is owned by the taxpayer, the spouse or jointly. Also, the Activity Information is essential in determining whether or not the activity should be treated as passive activity. The assumption is that the activity **is passive**, thus you enter an X (i.e. click on the mouse) if the activity is **NOT PASSIVE.** For real estate activities, you must indicate the level of participation -- material or active. Also, you must indicate if the activity is a qualified low-income housing activity. This information is used in applying and reporting the passive activities of the taxpayer. It is important. If you are uncertain of the terms, use the *Help* button.

PASSIVE ACTIVITIES

If you have gains or losses from passive activities (including prior year disallowed losses), you must file Form 8582. (There are some exceptions that are indicated on the form.) Form 8582 is used to calculate the amount of loss from passive activities that is allowed on your tax return. TurboTax prepares Form 8582 automatically, that is all entries on Form 8582 are based on information from the Passive Activity Worksheets and other forms in your tax return. There are six passive activity worksheets which are used to limit passive activity losses on an activity-by-activity basis.

The flow of information to the Passive Activity Worksheets is controlled by the information you provide on other tax forms. As noted above, the key questions that appear on the Schedule K-1s and other forms are:

1. Check if Material Participation -- If yes then the ordinary income or loss from trade or business activities are not passive activities; otherwise, they are included as passive activities and summarized on the Passive Activities Worksheets that are summarized on Form 8582.

2. Check if Active Participation in the operation of the activity -- If you check here, the real estate activities up to the applicable limits are not considered passive.

3. Check if Complete Disposition -- Checking indicates that you have disposed of the property and are entitled to all current and deferred losses. Not checking indicates that you still own the property and are therefore still subject to the passive activity loss limitations.

Careful consideration of your answers to these questions on the various forms will insure you that Form 8582 will be completed for all current passive activities. The forms, schedules and worksheets that will transfer amounts to the Passive Activity Loss Worksheets are listed below for your information.

- Schedules C, E, and F
- Form 6252, Installment Sales
- K-1 Worksheets for Partnerships, S Corporations, and Estates and Trusts
- Worksheet for Federal Income Tax Carryover Data

The major problem you will have is the addition of carryover information that is not included on the Worksheet for Federal Income Tax Carryover Data. If you used TurboTax in the prior year, the **File Transfer** option will correctly add any carryover amounts to the carryover worksheet and from there to the various schedules that report the activity. However, if this is the first year that you have used TurboTax, the appropriate information relating to the passive loss carryovers must be added to this year's return. Carryovers can be added to the activity's schedule, Schedule C, K-1 Worksheet, at the end of the worksheet, etc. If you are using TurboTax's **EasyStep**, it will walk you through the appropriate questions. If you get stuck using the Forms Method, select **EasyStep** and let TurboTax do the work. You can press **F1** along the way to display information to help you answer the questions. These help screens are useful; use them.

The bottom-line is that if you correctly answer the required questions, TurboTax will complete Form 8582 for current year's transactions. If there are no carryovers, that's it. If you have carryovers, they must be correctly entered on either the K-1 worksheet or other activity worksheet.

SELF-EMPLOYMENT INCOME

Self-employment income from partnerships is reported on K-1s. In entering the income on the K-1 worksheets, you must be certain to enter the income on line 15a **and** on line 15b or 15c in order to correctly compute the Self-employment tax. Self-employment income from sole proprietorships is transferred from Schedule C to the appropriate line on Schedule SE. TurboTax does the work for you. If you reported the amounts correctly, the self-employment income and related tax will be correctly computed.

ALTERNATIVE MINIMUM TAX

Form 6251 must be completed to report all amounts that may result in an Alternative Minimum Tax. TurboTax calculates much of the form automatically, although you may need to OVERRIDE certain lines on Form 6251 if your tax situation involves an exception or a special case. One type of special case is the occurrence of a loss from an activity where the taxpayer is not at-risk. TurboTax does not check if an asset was used in an activity for which you are not at-risk. Thus, you may be required to use the OVERRIDE option to adjust the loss amount if you are not at-risk. You may have to make some entries for amounts not picked up by the program (i.e. those fields on Form 6251 that are "Enter Amount" fields).

The major point is that TurboTax is going to correctly transfer the required amounts from other forms to Form 6251. For those situations where there are questions about how to report AMT related transactions, use the EasyStep to get help. For most taxpayers, you will only have to explain the tax to the taxpayer. TurboTax can figure it out.

PENALTY FOR UNDERPAYMENT OF ESTIMATED TAX

TurboTax will compute the penalty for underpayment of estimated tax reported on Form 2210. The computation is based upon payment amounts you entered on the W-2 Worksheets, Carryover Worksheet, and the Form 1040. The program also uses the information you enter on Form 2210. TurboTax and the IRS assume that all estimated tax payment amounts were equal over the year. If they were not, you have to check the appropriate box on Form 2210 and use the OVERRIDE command to enter the Quarterly amounts. The IRS encourages that you do not file Form 2210. Instead the IRS will compute the penalty and bill the taxpayer. As noted on Form 2210 there are four exceptions. If you are required to file Form 2210, TurboTax will support its preparation. As a real world warning, in the past, the IRS has been notorious for computing unusual amounts as penalty taxes. This is one area of tax where "To err is human. To really foul things up requires an IRS computer." Fortunately, TurboTax does better.

WHERE CAN YOU GET MORE SUPPORT?

If after reading this manual, looking at the Help features, and asking your friend in the course, you still are having trouble using TurboTax, there is support straight from the horse's mouth, so to speak. If all else fails, you can call the TurboTax Support group for help. The TurboTax Support Group can be reached by calling:

Technical Support Group (520) 295-3239
Monday - Friday, 8:30 AM - 5:00 PM PACIFIC TIME

Another source of help is to surf the Internet. Intuit supports a web page referred to as the "Quicken Financial Network." The URL is

http://www.intuit.com

Part of this web page is Frequently Asked Questions where you can get substantial information about TurboTax. There is an e-mail link for you to ask questions directly to the support staff. They will answer by e-mail also.

When you call, be certain that you know what type of PC you are using, the type of printer, disk drives, processor, and that you know what error messages you received if any. The people in the installation group are very patient, but they need this information if they are to be able to help you solve the problem. It is also extremely helpful if you can be sitting at your PC, with the PC up and running when you call. For more information about the customer service available from Intuit, also look at the next chapter.

CONCLUDING COMMENTS

All the command options available with TurboTax for Windows have been discussed. As stated along the way, TurboTax will help you prepare a tax return, but it will not make tax decisions for you. You will need to study the tax law in order to know how to treat the various transactions that occur during a normal year. The program is forms oriented and provides help in identifying the forms that you need for certain transactions. You will still need to summarize the transactions for the year and to be aware of which transactions to pursue further.

As with any software, you need to use it to learn it. In Chapter 6 you are provided with practice problems and some solutions. In addition, the first problem gives you a step-by-step walk through the use of TurboTax. Regardless of your level of knowledge about using the personal computer, I assure you that you can use TurboTax to prepare a tax return. Go for it!

CHAPTER 5

CUSTOMER SERVICE FROM TURBOTAX

TurboTax software included with this manual is the version that is distributed by Intuit for personal use. All TurboTax users, including students and faculty, are eligible to obtain support from experts at Intuit. Support is available if difficulties are encountered while installing or using TurboTax and the user is unable to rectify the situation after reading this manual and searching the TurboTax Help options. The purpose of this chapter is to identify Intuit customer services. Note, however, that you should not rely on TurboTax support to answer questions concerning tax law arising from tax course assignments.

If you have difficulty using TurboTax

First, don't panic. Think through the steps you have just followed. There are resources available to help you. If there is an error message on your screen, write it on a sheet of paper for later reference.

Steps for solving TurboTax technical difficulties are as follows:

1. Consult this manual, Program Help, and the READ1040 file, discussed in Chapter 2.
2. Confirm that your computer conforms to the system requirements discussed in Chapter 2.
3. If you are still having trouble, connect to the Intuit web site (www.intuit.com) or call the Intuit toll-free automated technical support services at 1-800-685-7369.

TurboTax Web site http://www.turbotax.com

TurboTax technical support is available from the World Wide Web 24 hours a day. The TurboTax Web site is constantly updated and offers:

1. Technical support information and answers to frequently asked questions
2. Downloadable program updates
3. Late-breaking tax and product news
4. TurboTax federal and state product information
5. Downloadable TurboTax State software

TurboTax includes Internet Explorer Intuit Edition software to facilitate connection to the TurboTax Web site. If you installed Internet Explorer or if you already have a web browser on your computer, go to the TurboTax Help menu and click on TurboTax Web Site to access the site. Consider making a web "bookmark" for the site for future reference.

Automated technical support (800) 685-7369

Toll-free automated technical support (ATS) provides recordings of frequently asked questions, technical support tips, late-breaking news about TurboTax, and product updates. Information is constantly updated.

To use ATS, you need a touch-tone telephone, a pen or pencil, and a piece of paper.

1. ATS asks you a series of questions to which you respond by pressing telephone keys.
2. Based on information you provide, ATS provides possible solutions
3. You can save your ATS session, then return to it after you try the proposed solution

   If you save your ATS session (ATS tells you how), ATS provides a case number. Write down the case number. The next time you call, enter the case number and ATS retrieves the session in progress; that way you don't have to start your session over at the beginning.

Tip *If you have access to a fax machine or fax modem, you can have recorded ATS information sent to you by fax. ATS tells you how.*

Technical support representatives (520) 295-3239

Regular Hours: Monday through Friday, 8:30 a.m. to 5:00 p.m., Pacific Time.

Extended Hours: December 29, 1997 through April 15, 1998
Monday through Sunday, 5:00 a.m. - 10:00 p.m., Pacific Time.

Fax-on-demand service (800) 766-5034

If you have a fax machine or a fax modem, use Intuit's toll-free Fax service for frequently asked questions, technical support tips, late-breaking news about TurboTax, and product updates. Fax documents are constantly updated.

Before you call, write down your area code and fax number and have them in front of you.

1. **Call (800) 766-5034.**
   TaxFax gives you instructions on how to choose either a particular document that applies to your situation or a catalog that lists all available document topics.

2. **At the prompt, choose to receive either a particular document or the catalog of documents.**
   You can request up to three documents at a time.

3. **At the prompt, enter your fax number and phone number.**
   Remain on the line while the system processes your request. The line automatically disconnects, and the requested documents are faxed to you, usually within minutes of your call. If you do not receive your documents within four hours of your call, call and make your request again.

How do I find a professional tax advisor?

While not appropriate for typical tax course assignments, the Intuit Financial Professional Network can help you find tax experts in your geographic area. Access the Intuit Web site (www.intuit.com) for more information.

CHAPTER 6

TAX RETURN PROBLEMS

The purpose of this chapter is to provide tax return problems for your use in learning TurboTax for Windows. Problems move you through many, but not all, of the forms used with TurboTax for Windows. You may encounter some transactions that have not been covered in your tax course. Welcome to the real world. One of the strengths of TurboTax for Windows is its help features, both Tax Help and Program Help. You are encouraged to use HELP features while you are preparing the return.

Names and other tax data in all problems are fictitious. Any resemblance to specific individuals is purely coincidental.

Tax forms ask questions that are designed to aid in the audit of a wide variety of transactions. Accordingly, several questions apply in only limited circumstances. If the problem information does not address one of the questions, leave the answer blank. Make no entry of any kind unless instructed otherwise by your professor. The risk in guessing at such entries is that you may mark a transaction for special treatment by TurboTax for Windows.

Problems 1 and 2 are followed by complete solutions. Problem 1 is followed by step-by-step instructions to complete the problem, thereby providing a guided tour of TurboTax for Windows. These solutions were prepared using the same version of the software that is included with this manual.

In your search for more problems, remember that your tax textbook likely includes tax form problems that may also be completed with TurboTax. As with any complex task, the more practice you have, the more skilled you will become.

PROBLEM 1 Mary Brown

Objective: Sample problem and solution. Taxable scholarship, unreported tip income and related FICA tax.

Mary Brown is an accounting major at the University of Michigan who is single and works in the summer as a waitress for the Michigan House, the premier restaurant in Acme. Mary was born September 20, 1976. She presents you with the following information:

Social security number	345-23-4567
Address	345 Florida Ave., Acme, MI 49610
Home telephone number	313-555-5555
Employer	Michigan House, One Main Street, employer number 65-76543256
Wages	$ 2,345
Federal income taxes W/H	$ 0
State income taxes W/H	$ 0
Social security taxes	$ 145
Medicare taxes	$ 34

In addition, Mary received $680 in interest income from the Bank of Acme. Mary has no interest from any other accounts.

In reviewing her records, Mary discovered that she had failed to report $45 of tip income received during August, her last month of work.

Mary received an $8,000 scholarship at the University. She expended the funds as follows: $6,000 for tuition, $500 for books and required supplies, and $1,500 for dormitory charges.

Mary lived at home during the summer. Her parents gave her a car (it cost her parents $8,000) to drive to work in Acme and to use while at school. In addition, they gave her $3,000 to cover food, clothing, and other expenses at school. If possible, Mary's parents plan to claim her as a dependent. Mary supports the Presidential Election Campaign Fund and does want $3 to go to that fund.

REQUIRED: Complete Mary's federal income tax return.

STEP-BY-STEP SOLUTION

The following pages provide a step-by-step solution of this problem using the **EasyStep Approach**.

STEP 1: Load TurboTax.

Refer to the installation procedures in Chapter 2. To load the program, double click on the red, white and blue top hat that is the icon for TurboTax for Windows. If you are using Windows 95, click on the Start button, move the mouse pointer to "Programs," and then to the TurboTax 1997 folder, and then to the TurboTax icon titled "TurboTax 1997 for Windows." Click to load TurboTax.

STEP 2: Select **EasyStep** Method

You are welcomed to TurboTax. After reading your welcome, click on Next **twice**. Then you have the opportunity to select from "Two Ways to Do Your Taxes," as shown in Figure 3-1 in Chapter 3. Click on "Next" to continue with EasyStep. Then you will see the "Track your Progress" screen showing the first few steps in EasyStep. Click on Next.

You now are able to transfer data from last year's return. Since this problem does not provide data from last year, click on "Continue this return."

You are given the opportunity to **Import** data from Quicken, Quickbooks or other accounting software. Unfortunately, you will have to "Skip" this option. Mary does not use any accounting software. Click on Next. You can skip the commercial for now by clicking Next.

STEP 3: Tutorial

Click on the button "Tell me how this works" for an on-screen tutorial about the EasyStep Method. It is brief and you are strongly encouraged to work through the tutorial before proceeding.

STEP 4: Pre-interview screens

Click on the button "Let's get started." Next, you can view additional tutorials. Doing so is optional. Click on Next to proceed. You will then be asked if you want to file your return electronically. Since this is an academic exercise, you should click on No. You will then be asked if you want to file your return using the 1040PC format. Click on No. **Finally**, click on the button "Yourself" to indicate that you are taking the role of a single taxpayer, Mary Brown. Then, click on Next.

STEP 5: Interview

You are now ready to begin entering tax return data. As shown in Figure 6-1, enter Mary Brown in the appropriate input areas on your screen.

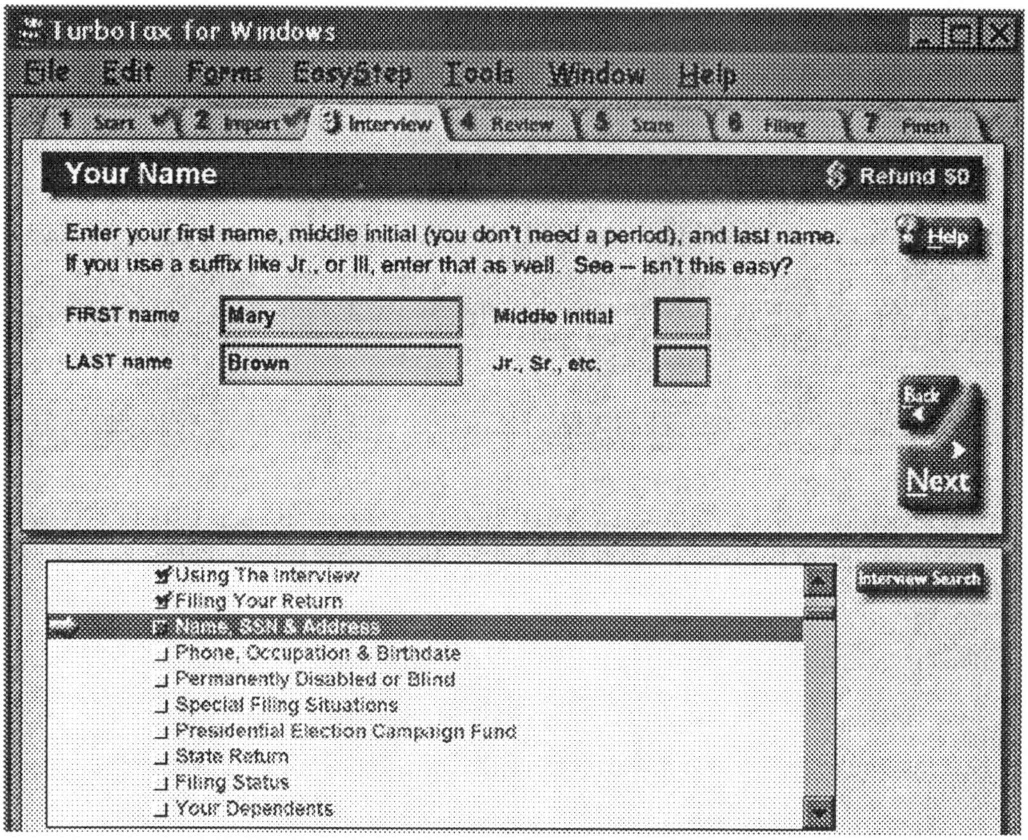

Figure 6-1 Entering the taxpayer's name

Next, click on the "View Current Form" tab at the bottom of the screen. You will then see Mary Brown's name appear on the TurboTax Federal Information Worksheet, from which the tax return will be electronically prepared. Once enough data are entered, you will see actual filled-in tax forms in the lower part of your screen. Viewing the forms in this manner will help you learn how they are prepared and how one form relates to others.

As you continue to answer questions in the top part of the screen, data will be entered on the form displayed in the lower part of the screen. Enter Mary's social security number, address, etc. Press the Next button when you are ready to proceed to the next screen. (Rather than pressing Next, the next screen will automatically appear if you press the Enter key after entering the last input item on a screen.)

Note that you can edit and/or add information in the bottom half of the screen by clicking on an item. Thus, an alternative to answering questions in the top half of the screen is to enter information directly on the forms in the bottom half of the screen.

Why does TurboTax ask for your phone number, your birthday, and other information seemingly unrelated to tax return preparation? The reason is that many state returns require it. Your birthday is important so TurboTax can determine if you are over 65, or over 25 for the Earned Income Credit.

When entering birthdays, you must enter in the form mm/dd/yy. You can enter the slashes but TurboTax will include them automatically if you do not. If you have a single-digit month or day, you must precede with the number with a zero. Thus, September 20, 1996 is entered as 092096.

Now comes a series of questions. When you do not have the requested information, leave it blank. If you are not certain of the answer, take the default answer — the one with the light, white dotted line on the button.

Permanently disabled?	NO
Exemption for Blindness?	NO
Someone's Dependent?	Tax knowledge is necessary here. Very briefly, Mary meets the relationship test, gross income test (student exception); support test (car counts but scholarship does not count); joint return test, and residency test. Thus, Mary can be claimed as someone's dependent. If you were not certain, you could click on **Help,** and TurboTax would give you the tax law.
Presidential Election Fund?	YES - Problem says Mary does support this fund.
Filing state return?	NO

Taxpayer information is now complete. Click on Next.

But the questions continue. Filing status? TurboTax offers to guide you through this question. In Mary's case, Single is the only status that can apply. Check to see that it is selected and click on Next. EasyStep explains why you should consider saving the file frequently and then tells you that you will be given several opportunities to do so. Take them.

Your are asked more questions. Dependents? NO. Mini-Review? Click on it — Hurrah! No errors! Now the Personal Information Worksheet is complete. Click on Next.

TurboTax gives you the option to take the "Fast Track," or do the "Entire Course." For this time, and this time only, I suggest that you take the entire course -- all 60 (more or less) questions.

The first question is "Do you have W-2 forms?" Yes. Information about wages, taxes withheld, social security wages, social security taxes, medicare wages, medicare taxes, and state income taxes given in the problem would be reported on a W-2 form. TurboTax will prompt you for the numbers. Enter as asked. Note, the Social Security wages are generally equal to the Wages. They can be different if certain fringe benefits are provided, or if the wages are over the limit of $65,400 for 1997. Also, Medicare wages are normally the same as the wages. After you have entered the Medicare tax, there are no more numbers to enter on the W-2. You are asked about Boxes 13-15, but these do not apply to Mary, so skip them. Select the "Done with . . . ." options. Then you are asked about state wages and withholding. State wages are the same as federal and Mary's state withholdings are 0.

There is no information to add until you reach the first Interest screen. Mary does have $680 interest income. Click as directed to indicate the interest is taxable (since it is from a savings account). Enter the payer's name and the amount. Click on Next. Then answer No to questions about other types of interest and accounts.

Then you are asked about various types of other income including Form 1099 income. Answer No to them. Ultimately, you will arrive at the "Your Income -- Mini-Review" screen. Click on the Mini-Review button to review your income inputs. Then, continue by clicking Next.

You will be asked about various categories of business income. Mary has none. Just answer No until you reach the "Miscellaneous Income" screen. Note that one of the examples of miscellaneous income is taxable scholarships and fellowships. Mary's scholarship is partially taxable. Since $1,500 of the $8,000 scholarship was not spent on tuition, books or supplies, the $1,500 is taxable (even though it was spent for room and board). Thus, click Yes twice and enter 1500 in the appropriate space.

Continue to answer No or Next to proceed. Soon you will arrive at the "Adjusted Gross Income" (AGI) screen which should report that Mary's AGI is $4,525. Click Next.

You are given the option to itemize deductions; say No. Mary uses the standard deduction. Note that at the right side of the title bar, it is noted that you have "Tax Due $103." After all, Mary has no withholding taxes. Click on No and Next as you proceed through other items that may impact a tax return. Note that Mary is not eligible for any tax credits.

You are given an opportunity to consider if Mary is subject to the Alternative Minimum Tax. If you have covered that topic in class, take a look at Form 6251. Otherwise, skip this opportunity by answering No.

You will answer several additional questions about sources of income, none of which Mary has. So, just answer No. When you come to "**Unreported Tips**," stop. Recall that Mary failed (forgot?) to report $45 in tips last August. Even though it is not much money, it is still subject to taxes. So, answer Yes. Recall that the text in blue and underlined, is hypertext. Thus, if you want to know more about which tips must be reported, click on the blue phrase and learn. Note that Form 4137, for unreported tip income, is automatically completed by TurboTax based on the information already entered. You can view Form 4137 by clicking on the "View Current Form" tab at the bottom of the screen. Note the tax is $4. Continue clicking through screens. You will be asked to enter the employer's name.

Complete the interview process by clicking either No or Next. As mentioned earlier, do **NOT** choose to print the return in **1040PC Format** (unless your are instructed to do so by your instructor). When you reach the screen titled, "That's all folks," your tax return is complete. Congratulations!

Now, all that is left is to save the file and print the return. To save the file, just click on File (located in the upper left-hand corner of the screen). Then, click on Save. To print, click on Filing, the sixth tab in the upper right-hand corner of your screen. Then, in the bottom half of the screen, click on "Print Conventional." The screen title in the upper half of the screen should now be "Print a Copy to File with IRS." Click on Next and the return will print.

To terminate your session with TurboTax, click on the Finish tab in the upper right-hand corner of the TurboTax screen. Then click on Next and then the "Exit TurboTax" button. (A window may appear regarding saving your file.)

The following pages include a completed tax return for Mary Brown. Note that TurboTax decides what form to file (1040, 1040A, or 1040EZ.) You do not have to choose. Mary has to file Form 1040 because she has social security tax due on unreported tip income. Form 1040 provides Line 47 for that purpose.

Note that the preparer line indicates that the return was "Self-prepared." Recall that this is the personal 1040 version of TurboTax for Windows and by license agreement, it may not be used by paid preparers. The Pro Series is designed for tax return preparers. For class purposes, just write your name to the right of "Self-prepared" and hand it in. Note that the IRS requires a payment voucher, Form 1040V, to accompany any tax payment.

What's Next?

Consider working either problem 2 or 3, next. All related tax forms are included in this book for your reference. Only your instructor has access to solutions for other problems.

Mary Brown
345 Florida Ave.
Acme, MN 49610

1997 U. S. INDIVIDUAL INCOME TAX RETURN SUMMARY

Adjusted Gross Income	$	4,570
Taxable Income	$	680
Total Tax	$	107
Total Payments	$	0
Payment Due IRS	$	107
Tax Bracket		15.00 %

INSTRUCTIONS FOR MAILING YOUR RETURN

Your federal Form 1040 shows a tax due of $107. Include a check or money order for this amount, payable to the Internal Revenue Service. Write your social security number and '1997 Form 1040' on the check. Please mail your return to the following IRS address postmarked by Wednesday, April 15, 1998.

Internal Revenue Service
Kansas City, MO 64999-0002

Be sure to sign and date your return and include the proper amount of postage on the envelope.

Department of the Treasury — Internal Revenue Service

Form 1040 U.S. Individual Income Tax Return 1997

(99) IRS use only — Do not write or staple in this space.

For the year Jan 1 - Dec 31, 1997, or other tax year beginning , 1997, ending , 19 OMB No. 1545-0074

Label (See instructions.)

Use the IRS label. Otherwise, please print or type.

Your First Name	MI	Last Name	Your Social Security No.
Mary		Brown	345-23-4567
If a Joint Return, Spouse's First Name	MI	Last Name	Spouse's Social Security No.
Home Address (number and street). If You Have a P.O. Box, See Instructions.		Apartment No.	For help finding line instructions, see instructions in the booklet.
345 Florida Ave.			
City, Town or Post Office. If You Have a Foreign Address, See Instructions.	State	ZIP Code	
Acme	MN	49610	

Presidential Election Campaign (See instructions.)

	Yes	No	
Do you want 3 to go to this fund?	X		Note: Checking 'Yes' will not change your tax or reduce your refund.
If a joint return, does your spouse want 3 to go to this fund?			

Filing Status

Check only one box.

1 [X] Single
2 [ ] Married filing joint return (even if only one had income)
3 [ ] Married filing separate return. Enter spouse's SSN above & full name here ... ▶
4 [ ] Head of household (with qualifying person). (See instructions.) If the qualifying person is a child but not your dependent, enter this child's name here ... ▶
5 [ ] Qualifying widow(er) with dependent child (year spouse died ▶ 19). (See instructions.)

Exemptions

6a [ ] **Yourself.** If your parent (or someone else) can claim you as a dependent on his or her tax return, **do not** check box 6a .... No. of boxes checked on 6a and 6b .....

b [ ] **Spouse** ....

c **Dependents:**

If more than six dependents, see instructions.

(1) First name	Last name	(2) Dependent's social security number	(3) Dependent's relationship to you	(4) No. of months lived in your home in 1997

No. of your children on 6c who:
• lived with you ......
• did not live with you due to divorce or separation (see instructions) ..
Dependents on line 6c not entered above ....
Add numbers entered on lines above ▶

d Total number of exemptions claimed ....

Income

Attach Copy B of your Forms W-2, W-2G, & 1099-R here.

If you did not get a W-2, see instructions.

Enclose, but do not attach, any payment. Also, please use Form 1040-V.

7	Wages, salaries, tips, etc. Attach Form(s) W-2.... SCH, 1500	7: 3,890.
8a	**Taxable** interest. Attach Schedule B if required	8a: 680.
b	**Tax-exempt** interest. **Do not** include on line 8a ... 8b	
9	Dividends. Attach Schedule B if required	9
10	Taxable refunds, credits, or offsets of state and local income taxes (see instructions)	10
11	Alimony received	11
12	Business income or (loss). Attach Schedule C or C-EZ	12
13	Capital gain or (loss). Attach Schedule D	13
14	Other gains or (losses). Attach Form 4797	14
15a	Total IRA distributions ... 15a — b Taxable amount (see instrs)	15b
16a	Total pensions and annuities ... 16a — b Taxable amount (see instrs)	16b
17	Rental real estate, royalties, partnerships, S corporations, trusts, etc. Attach Schedule E	17
18	Farm income or (loss). Attach Schedule F	18
19	Unemployment compensation	19
20a	Social security benefits ... 20a — b Taxable amount (see instrs)	20b
21	Other income. List type and amount — see instructions	21
22	Add the amounts in the far right column for lines 7 - 21. This is your **total income** ▶	22: 4,570.

Adjusted Gross Income

If line 32 is under 29,290 (under 9,770 if a child did not live with you), see EIC in the instructions.

23	IRA deduction (see instructions)	23
24	Medical savings account deduction. Attach Form 8853	24
25	Moving expenses. Attach Form 3903 or 3903-F	25
26	One-half of self-employment tax. Attach Schedule SE	26
27	Self-employed health insurance deduction (see instructions)	27
28	Keogh and self-employed SEP and SIMPLE plans	28
29	Penalty on early withdrawal of savings	29
30a	Alimony paid. b Recipient's SSN ▶	30a
31	Add lines 23 - 30a	31
32	Subtract line 31 from line 22. This is your **adjusted gross income** ▶	32: 4,570.

BAA For Privacy Act and Paperwork Reduction Act Notice, see instructions. Form 1040 (1997)

FDIA0112 10/24/97

Tax Computation

Line	Description	Box	Amount
33	Amount from line 32 (adjusted gross income)	33	4,570.
34a	Check if: ☐ You were 65/older, ☐ Blind; ☐ Spouse was 65/older, ☐ Blind. Add the number of boxes checked above and enter the total here ▶	34a	
b	If you are married filing separately and your spouse itemizes deductions or you were a dual-status alien, see instructions and check here ▶	34b ☐	
35	Enter the larger of your: **Itemized deductions** from Schedule A, line 28, **Or** **Standard deduction** shown below for your filing status. **But** see the instructions if you checked any box on line 34a or 34b **or** someone can claim you as a dependent. • Single – 4,150 • Married filing jointly or Qualifying widow(er) – 6,900 • Head of household – 6,050 • Married filing separately – 3,450	35	3,890.
36	Subtract line 35 from line 33	36	680.
37	If line 33 is $90,900 or less, multiply $2,650 by the total number of exemptions claimed on line 6d. If line 33 is over $90,900, see the worksheet in the instructions for the amount to enter	37	0.
38	**Taxable income.** Subtract line 37 from line 36. If line 37 is more than line 36, enter -0-	38	680.
39	**Tax.** See instrs. Check if any tax from a ☐ Form(s) 8814 b ☐ Form 4972 ▶	39	103.

If you want the IRS to figure your tax, see instructions.

Credits

Line	Description	Box	Amount
40	Credit for child and dependent care expenses. Attach Form 2441	40	
41	Credit for the elderly or the disabled. Attach Sch R	41	
42	Adoption credit. Attach Form 8839	42	
43	Foreign tax credit. Attach Form 1116	43	
44	Other. Check if from a ☐ Form 3800 b ☐ Form 8396 c ☐ Form 8801 d ☐ Form (specify) ______	44	
45	Add lines 40 through 44	45	
46	Subtract line 45 from line 39. If line 45 is more than line 39, enter -0- ▶	46	103.

Other Taxes

Line	Description	Box	Amount
47	Self-employment tax. Attach Schedule SE	47	
48	Alternative minimum tax. Attach Form 6251	48	
49	SS and Medicare tax on tip income not reported to employer. Attach Form 4137	49	4.
50	Tax on qualified retirement plans (including IRAs) and MSAs. Attach Form 5329 if required	50	
51	Advance earned income credit payments from Form(s) W-2	51	
52	Household employment taxes. Attach Schedule H	52	
53	Add lns 46 - 52. This is your **total tax** ▶	53	107.

Payments

Attach Forms W-2, W-2G, and 1099-R to page 1.

Line	Description	Box	Amount
54	Federal income tax withheld from Forms W-2 and 1099	54	
55	1997 estimated tax payments and amount applied from 1996 return	55	
56a	**Earned income credit.** Attach Schedule EIC if you have a qualifying child. b Nontaxable earned income: amount ▶ ______ and type ▶ ______	56a	No
57	Amount paid with Form 4868 (request for extension)	57	
58	Excess social security and RRTA tax withheld (see instrs)	58	
59	Other payments. Check if from a ☐ Form 2439 b ☐ Form 4136	59	
60	Add lines 54, 55, 56a, 57, 58, and 59. These are your **total payments** ▶	60	

Refund

Have it directly deposited! See instructions and fill in 62b, 62c, and 62d.

Line	Description	Box	Amount
61	If line 60 is more than line 53, subtract line 53 from line 60. This is the amount you **Overpaid**	61	
62a	Amount of line 61 you want **Refunded to You** ▶	62a	
▶ b	Routing number ______ c Type: ☐ Checking ☐ Savings		
▶ d	Account number ______		
63	Amount of line 61 you want **Applied to Your 1998 Estimated Tax** ▶	63	

Amount You Owe

Line	Description	Box	Amount
64	If line 53 is more than line 60, subtract line 60 from line 53. This is the **Amount You Owe.** For details on how to pay, see instructions ▶	64	107.
65	Estimated tax penalty. Also include on line 64	65	

Sign Here

Under penalties of perjury, I declare that I have examined this return and accompanying schedules and statements, and to the best of my knowledge and belief, they are true, correct, and complete. Declaration of preparer (other than taxpayer) is based on all information of which preparer has any knowledge.

Keep a copy of this return for your records.

Your Signature	Date	Your Occupation
▶		waitress
Spouse's Signature. If a Joint Return, BOTH Must Sign.	**Date**	**Spouse's Occupation**
▶		

Paid Preparer's Use Only

Preparer's Signature ▶	Date	Check if self-employed ☐	Preparer's Social Security No.
Firm's Name (or yours if self-employed) and Address ▶ Self-prepared		EIN	
		ZIP Code	

Name(s) Shown on Form 1040. Do Not Enter Name and Social Security Number if Shown on Schedule A. | Your Social Security Number

Mary Brown | 345-23-4567

Schedule B – Interest and Dividend Income

08

Part I Interest Income

(See instructions.)

Note: If you received a Form 1099-INT, Form 1099-OID, or substitute statement from a brokerage firm, list the firm's name as the payer and enter the total interest shown on that form.

Note: *If you had over 400 in taxable interest income, you must also complete Part III.*

			Amount
1	List name of payer. If any interest is from a seller-financed mortgage and the buyer used the property as a personal residence, see the instructions and list this interest first. Also, show that buyer's social security number and address ►	1	
	Bank of Acme		680.00
2	Add the amounts on line 1	2	680.00
3	Excludable interest on series EE U.S. savings bonds issued after 1989 from Form 8815, line 14. You **must** attach Form 8815 to Form 1040	3	
4	Subtract line 3 from line 2. Enter the result here and on Form 1040, line 8a ►	4	680.00

Part II Dividend Income

(See instructions.)

Note: If you received a Form 1099-DIV, or substitute statement from a brokerage firm, list the firm's name as the payer and enter the total dividends shown on that form.

Note: *If you had over 400 in gross dividends and/or other distributions on stock, you must also complete Part III.*

			Amount
5	List name of payer. Include gross dividends and/or other distributions on stock here. Any capital gain distributions and nontaxable distributions will be deducted on lines 7 and 8 ►	5	
6	Add the amounts on line 5	6	
7	Capital gain distributions. Enter here and on Schedule D — 7		
8	Nontaxable distributions. (See the instructions for Form 1040, line 9.) — 8		
9	Add lines 7 and 8	9	
10	Subtract line 9 from line 6. Enter the result here and on Form 1040, line 9 ►	10	

Part III Foreign Accounts and Trusts

(See instructions.)

You must complete this part if you **(a)** had over 400 of interest or dividends; **(b)** had a foreign account; or **(c)** received a distribution from, or were a grantor of, or a transferor to, a foreign trust.

		Yes	No
11a	At any time during 1997, did you have an interest in or a signature or other authority over a financial account in a foreign country, such as a bank account, securities account, or other financial account? See instructions for exceptions and filing requirements for Form TD F 90-22.1		X
b	If 'yes,' enter the name of the foreign country ►		
12	During 1997, did you receive a distribution from, or were you the grantor of, or transferor to, a foreign trust? If 'yes,' you may have to file Form 3520 or 926. See instructions		X

Form **4137**

Department of the Treasury
Internal Revenue Service

Social Security and Medicare Tax on Unreported Tip Income

► See instructions.
► Attach to Form 1040.

OMB No. 1545-0059

1997

24

Name of Person Who Received Tips (as shown on Form 1040). If Married, Complete a Separate Form 4137 for Each Spouse with Unreported Tips.: Mary Brown

Social Security Number: 345-23-4567

Name(s) of Employer(s) to Whom You Were Required to, but Did Not, Report Your Tips:

Michigan House

Line	Description			Box	Amount
1	Total cash and charge tips you **received** in 1997			1	45.
2	Total cash and charge tips you **reported** to your employer in 1997			2	
3	Subtract line 2 from line 1. This amount is income you **must** include in the total on Form 1040, line 7			3	45.
4	Cash and charge tips you received but did not report to your employer because the total was less than 20 in a calendar month			4	
5	Unreported tips subject to Medicare tax. Subtract line 4 from line 3. Enter here and on line 2 of Schedule U below			5	45.
6	Maximum amount of wages (including tips) subject to social security tax	6	65,400.		
7	Total social security wages and social security tips (total of boxes 3 and 7 on Form(s) W-2) or railroad retirement (tier 1) compensation	7	2,345.		
8	Subtract line 7 from line 6. If line 7 is more than line 6, enter -0- here and on line 9 and go to line 11			8	63,055.
9	Unreported tips subject to social security tax. Compare the amounts on lines 5 and 8 above. Enter the **smaller** of the two amounts here and on line 1 of Schedule U below. If you received tips as a federal, state, or local government employee, see instructions			9	45.
10	Multiply line 9 by .062			10	3.
11	Multiply line 5 by .0145			11	1.
12	Add lines 10 and 11. Enter the result here and on Form 1040, line 49 ►			12	4.

Form **4137** (1997)

Do Not Detach

Schedule U
(Form 1040)

Department of the Treasury
Internal Revenue Service

U.S. Schedule of Unreported Tip Income

For crediting to your social security record

1997

Note: *The amounts you report below are for your social security record. This record is used to figure any benefits, based on your earnings, payable to you and your dependents or your survivors. Fill in each item accurately and completely.*

Print or Type Name of Person Who Received Tip Income (as shown on Form 1040): Mary Brown

Social Security Number: 345-23-4567

Address (number and street, or P.O. box if mail is not delivered to your home): 345 Florida Ave.

Apartment No.:

Occupation: waitress

City, Town or Post Office: Acme

State: MN ZIP Code: 49610

1	Unreported tips subject to social security tax. Enter the amount from line 9 (Form 4137) above ►	1	45.
2	Unreported tips subject to Medicare tax. Enter the amount from line 5 (Form 4137) above ►	2	45.

Please do not write in this space

DLN–

BAA For Paperwork Reduction Act Notice, see separate instructions.

FDIA4001 11/05/97

Wages, Salaries, & Tips Worksheet 1997

► Keep for your records

Name(s) Shown on Return	Social Security Number
Mary Brown	345-23-4567

The following amounts are included in the total entered on line 7 of Form 1040 (or Form 1040A), on line 1 of Form 1040EZ, on line 8 of Form 1040NR:

		Taxpayer	Spouse	Total
1	Wages, from Form W-2	2,345.00		2,345.00
2	Miscellaneous income, Form 1099-MISC			
3	Disability or deferrals, from Form 1099-R			
4	Excess reimbursement, from Form 2106			
5	Taxable tips, from Form 4137	45.00		45.00
6	Excess moving expense reimbursement, from Form 3903 or 3903-F			
7	Wages earned as a household employee (if less than 1,000 and without a Form W-2)			
8	Sick pay or disability payments not on Form W-2 or Form 1099-R			
9	Other earned income			
10	**Subtotal. Add lines 1 through 9**	2,390.00		2,390.00
11	Taxable employer-provided dependent care benefits, from Form 2441 (or Schedule 2 of Form 1040A)			
12	Taxable employer-provided adoption benefits from Form 8839			
13	Scholarship/fellowship income not on Form W-2	1,500.00		1,500.00
14	Other			
15	**Total wages, salaries, tips, etc. Add lines 10 through 14**	3,890.00		3,890.00

PROBLEM 2 Larry and Pat Graham

Objective: Sample problem and solution. Joint return with child care, gain from sale of stock, and itemized deductions.

Larry Graham, is married to Pat Graham. Larry was born on July 10, 1949; Pat, on January 20, 1951. Larry works as a contract estimator for Madison Construction Co. Larry's W-2 reports the following information:

Address	456 Edgewood Ave., Madison WI 53706
Social security number	234-87-5643
Employer	Madison Construction Co., 432 Wisconsin
Wages	$34,000
Federal income taxes W/H	$ 3,454
State income taxes W/H	$ 2,080
Social security taxes	$ 2,108
Medicare taxes	$ 493

Pat is a stock broker with Mid-West Investors, and reports the following W-2 information:

Address	456 Edgewood Ave., Madison WI 53706
Social security number	243-12-3000
Employer	Mid-West Investors, 34 State Street, Madison,
Wages	$35,000
Federal income taxes W/H	$ 5,250
State income taxes W/H	$ 2,800
Social security taxes	$ 2,170
Medicare taxes	$ 507

The Grahams have two children: Larry, Jr. who is 5 months, and Michelle, who is 6 years old. Larry, Jr. SSN is 233-11-2311 and Michelle's social security number is 233-44-5566. Their telephone for state return purposes is 608-555-5555.

In addition to the salary income above, Larry and Pat incurred the following tax transactions:

1. Interest income from the Bank of Wisconsin, $455; interest income from State of Wisconsin bonds, $250.

2. Dividends were received on RayOVac Batteries stock of $345 and from Wisconsin Cheese Company of $125.

3. The Grahams had no interest in any foreign accounts or trusts.

4. Pat purchased 100 shares of Apple Computer stock on April 10, 1997 for $1,300. She sold the stock August 22, 1997 for $1,200.

5. Larry purchased 500 shares of SONY Inc. on March 5, 1987 for $22,500. He sold these also on August 22, 1997, for $30,000. The Grahams executed no other stock transactions during the year.

6. Child care for the Grahams' children was provided by Madison Care, 1299 Regent St., Madison, WI 53706, ID-Number 66-2345677. The Grahams paid $2,600 for care for both children.

7. The Grahams received a refund of Wisconsin income taxes of $85 in June of the current tax year. On their tax return filed last year, they had total itemized deductions of $14,300, which included $3,500 of state income taxes. Taxable income on that return was $48,700.

8. Potential itemized deductions for this year are the following:

   a. Real estate taxes, $1,000
   b. Personal property taxes based upon value of cars, $120
   c. Home mortgage interest reported on Form 1098, $7,400
   d. Interest on bank credit cards, $1,050
   e. Contributions to the University of Wisconsin, $1,500
   f. Fee for preparation of income tax returns, $450

9. Larry elects to support the Presidential Election Campaign Fund; Pat does not.

REQUIRED: Complete the federal income tax return.

Larry & Pat Graham
456 Edgewood Ave.
Madison, WI 53706

1997 U. S. INDIVIDUAL INCOME TAX RETURN SUMMARY

Adjusted Gross Income	$	77,410
Taxable Income	$	51,910
Total Tax	$	8,071
Total Payments	$	8,704
Refund	$	633
Tax Bracket		28.00 %

INSTRUCTIONS FOR MAILING YOUR RETURN

Your federal Form 1040 shows a refund of $633.
Please mail your return to the following IRS address postmarked by Wednesday, April 15, 1998.

Internal Revenue Service
Kansas City, MO 64999-0002

Be sure to sign and date your return and include the proper amount of postage on the envelope.

Please note, due to the tax law changes in Schedule D, the IRS will be holding all returns containing a Schedule D until their systems are updated in mid February. Schedule D returns will be processed beginning approximately February 11th.

Form **1040** Department of the Treasury — Internal Revenue Service
U.S. Individual Income Tax Return 1997 (99) IRS use only — Do not write or staple in this space.

For the year Jan 1 - Dec 31, 1997, or other tax year beginning , 1997, ending , 19 OMB No. 1545-0074

Label (See instructions.)	Your First Name: Larry	MI	Last Name: Graham	Your Social Security No.: 234-87-5643
Use the IRS label. Otherwise, please print or type.	If a Joint Return, Spouse's First Name: Pat	MI	Last Name: Graham	Spouse's Social Security No.: 243-12-3000
	Home Address (number and street). If You Have a P.O. Box, See Instructions.: 456 Edgewood Ave.	Apartment No.		**For help finding line instructions, see instructions in the booklet.**
	City, Town or Post Office. If You Have a Foreign Address, See Instructions.: Madison	State: WI	ZIP Code: 53706	

Presidential Election Campaign (See instructions.)

	Yes	No
Do you want 3 to go to this fund?	X	
If a joint return, does your spouse want 3 to go to this fund?		X

Note: Checking 'Yes' will not change your tax or reduce your refund.

Filing Status

Check only one box.

1 [ ] Single
2 [X] Married filing joint return (even if only one had income)
3 [ ] Married filing separate return. Enter spouse's SSN above & full name here ... ▶
4 [ ] Head of household (with qualifying person). (See instructions.) If the qualifying person is a child but not your dependent, enter this child's name here ... ▶
5 [ ] Qualifying widow(er) with dependent child (year spouse died ▶ 19). (See instructions.)

Exemptions

6a [X] **Yourself.** If your parent (or someone else) can claim you as a dependent on his or her tax return, **do not** check box 6a — No. of boxes checked on 6a and 6b: 2

b [X] **Spouse**

c **Dependents:**

(1) First name Last name	(2) Dependent's social security number	(3) Dependent's relationship to you	(4) No. of months lived in your home in 1997
Larry Graham Jr.	233-11-2311	Son	12
Michelle Graham	233-44-5566	Daughter	12

If more than six dependents, see instructions.

No. of your children on 6c who: ● lived with you: 2
● did not live with you due to divorce or separation (see instructions):
Dependents on line 6c not entered above:

d Total number of exemptions claimed — Add numbers entered on lines above ▶ 4

Income

Attach Copy B of your Forms W-2, W-2G, & 1099-R here.

If you did not get a W-2, see instructions.

Enclose, but do not attach, any payment. Also, please use **Form 1040-V.**

7	Wages, salaries, tips, etc. Attach Form(s) W-2	7	69,000.
8a	**Taxable** interest. Attach Schedule B if required	8a	455.
b	**Tax-exempt** interest. **Do not** include on line 8a — 8b: 250.		
9	Dividends. Attach Schedule B if required	9	470.
10	Taxable refunds, credits, or offsets of state and local income taxes (see instructions)	10	85.
11	Alimony received	11	
12	Business income or (loss). Attach Schedule C or C-EZ	12	
13	Capital gain or (loss). Attach Schedule D	13	7,400.
14	Other gains or (losses). Attach Form 4797	14	
15a	Total IRA distributions — 15a; b Taxable amount (see instrs)	15b	
16a	Total pensions and annuities — 16a; b Taxable amount (see instrs)	16b	
17	Rental real estate, royalties, partnerships, S corporations, trusts, etc. Attach Schedule E	17	
18	Farm income or (loss). Attach Schedule F	18	
19	Unemployment compensation	19	
20a	Social security benefits — 20a; b Taxable amount (see instrs)	20b	
21	Other income. List type and amount — see instructions	21	
22	Add the amounts in the far right column for lines 7 - 21. This is your **total income** ▶	22	77,410.

Adjusted Gross Income

If line 32 is under 29,290 (under 9,770 if a child did not live with you), see EIC in the instructions.

23	IRA deduction (see instructions)	23	
24	Medical savings account deduction. Attach Form 8853	24	
25	Moving expenses. Attach Form 3903 or 3903-F	25	
26	One-half of self-employment tax. Attach Schedule SE	26	
27	Self-employed health insurance deduction (see instructions)	27	
28	Keogh and self-employed SEP and SIMPLE plans	28	
29	Penalty on early withdrawal of savings	29	
30a	Alimony paid. b Recipient's SSN ▶	30a	
31	Add lines 23 - 30a	31	
32	Subtract line 31 from line 22. This is your **adjusted gross income** ▶	32	77,410.

BAA For Privacy Act and Paperwork Reduction Act Notice, see instructions. Form **1040** (1997)

Tax Computation

	33	Amount from line 32 (adjusted gross income)	33	77,410.
	34a	Check if: ☐ You were 65/older, ☐ Blind; ☐ Spouse was 65/older, ☐ Blind. Add the number of boxes checked above and enter the total here ▶ 34a		
	b	If you are married filing separately and your spouse itemizes deductions or you were a dual-status alien, see instructions and check here ▶ 34b ☐		
	35	Enter the larger of your: **Itemized deductions** from Schedule A, line 28, **Or** **Standard deduction** shown below for your filing status. **But** see the instructions if you checked any box on line 34a or 34b **or** someone can claim you as a dependent. • Single – 4,150 • Married filing jointly or Qualifying widow(er) – 6,900 • Head of household – 6,050 • Married filing separately – 3,450	35	14,900.
	36	Subtract line 35 from line 33	36	62,510.
If you want the IRS to figure your tax, see instructions.	37	If line 33 is $90,900 or less, multiply $2,650 by the total number of exemptions claimed on line 6d. If line 33 is over $90,900, see the worksheet in the instructions for the amount to enter	37	10,600.
	38	**Taxable income.** Subtract line 37 from line 36. If line 37 is more than line 36, enter -0-	38	51,910.
	39	**Tax.** See instrs. Check if any tax from a ☐ Form(s) 8814 b ☐ Form 4972 ▶	39	8,591.

Credits

40	Credit for child and dependent care expenses. Attach Form 2441	40	520.		
41	Credit for the elderly or the disabled. Attach Sch R	41			
42	Adoption credit. Attach Form 8839	42			
43	Foreign tax credit. Attach Form 1116	43			
44	Other. Check if from a ☐ Form 3800 b ☐ Form 8396 c ☐ Form 8801 d ☐ Form (specify) ______	44			
45	Add lines 40 through 44			45	520.
46	Subtract line 45 from line 39. If line 45 is more than line 39, enter -0- ▶			46	8,071.

Other Taxes

47	Self-employment tax. Attach Schedule SE	47	
48	Alternative minimum tax. Attach Form 6251	48	0.
49	SS and Medicare tax on tip income not reported to employer. Attach Form 4137	49	
50	Tax on qualified retirement plans (including IRAs) and MSAs. Attach Form 5329 if required	50	
51	Advance earned income credit payments from Form(s) W-2	51	
52	Household employment taxes. Attach Schedule H	52	
53	Add lns 46 - 52. This is your **total tax** ▶	53	8,071.

Payments

Attach Forms W-2, W-2G, and 1099-R to page 1.

54	Federal income tax withheld from Forms W-2 and 1099	54	8,704.		
55	1997 estimated tax payments and amount applied from 1996 return	55			
56a	**Earned income credit.** Attach Schedule EIC if you have a qualifying child. b Nontaxable earned income: amount ▶ ______ and type ▶ ______	56a			
57	Amount paid with Form 4868 (request for extension)	57			
58	Excess social security and RRTA tax withheld (see instrs)	58			
59	Other payments. Check if from a ☐ Form 2439 b ☐ Form 4136	59			
60	Add lines 54, 55, 56a, 57, 58, and 59. These are your **total payments** ▶			60	8,704.

Refund

Have it directly deposited! See instructions and fill in 62b, 62c, and 62d.

61	If line 60 is more than line 53, subtract line 53 from line 60. This is the amount you **Overpaid**	61	633.
62a	Amount of line 61 you want **Refunded to You** ▶	62a	633.
▶ b	Routing number ______ c Type: ☐ Checking ☐ Savings		
▶ d	Account number ______		
63	Amount of line 61 you want **Applied to Your 1998 Estimated Tax** ▶ 63		

Amount You Owe

64	If line 53 is more than line 60, subtract line 60 from line 53. This is the **Amount You Owe.** For details on how to pay, see instructions ▶	64	
65	Estimated tax penalty. Also include on line 64 — 65		

Sign Here

Under penalties of perjury, I declare that I have examined this return and accompanying schedules and statements, and to the best of my knowledge and belief, they are true, correct, and complete. Declaration of preparer (other than taxpayer) is based on all information of which preparer has any knowledge.

Keep a copy of this return for your records.

Your Signature	Date	Your Occupation
▶		Estimator
Spouse's Signature. If a Joint Return, BOTH Must Sign.	Date	Spouse's Occupation
▶		Stock Broker

Paid Preparer's Use Only

Preparer's Signature ▶	Date	Check if self-employed ☐	Preparer's Social Security No.
Firm's Name (or yours if self-employed) and Address ▶ Self-prepared		EIN	
		ZIP Code	

Schedule A (Form 1040)

Department of the Treasury Internal Revenue Service (99)

Itemized Deductions

► Attach to Form 1040.
► See Instructions for Schedule A (Form 1040).

OMB No. 1545-0074

1997

07

Name(s) Shown on Form 1040: Larry & Pat Graham

Your Social Security Number: 234-87-5643

Medical and Dental Expenses		**Caution:** *Do not include expenses reimbursed or paid by others.*				
	1	Medical and dental expenses (see instructions)	1			
	2	Enter amount from Form 1040, line 33 2				
	3	Multiply line 2 above by 7.5% (.075)	3			
	4	Subtract line 3 from line 1. If line 3 is more than line 1, enter -0-			4	
Taxes You Paid (See instructions.)	5	State and local income taxes	5	4,880.		
	6	Real estate taxes (see instructions)	6	1,000.		
	7	Personal property taxes	7	120.		
	8	Other taxes. List type and amount ►	8			
	9	Add lines 5 through 8			9	6,000.
Interest You Paid (See instructions.)	10	Home mortgage interest and points reported to you on Form 1098	10	7,400.		
	11	Home mortgage interest not reported to you on Form 1098. If paid to the person from whom you bought the home, see instructions and show that person's name, identifying number, and address ►	11			
Note: Personal interest is not deductible.	12	Points not reported to you on Form 1098. See instructions for special rules	12			
	13	Investment interest. Attach Form 4952 if required. (See instructions.)	13			
	14	Add lines 10 through 13			14	7,400.
Gifts to Charity	15	Gifts by cash or check. If you made any gift of 250 or more, see instructions	15	1,500.		
If you made a gift and got a benefit for it, see instructions.	16	Other than by cash or check. If any gift of 250 or more, see instructions. You **Must** attach Form 8283 if over 500	16			
	17	Carryover from prior year	17			
	18	Add lines 15 through 17			18	1,500.
Casualty and Theft Losses	19	Casualty or theft loss(es). Attach Form 4684. (See instructions.)			19	
Job Expenses and Most Other Miscellaneous Deductions	20	Unreimbursed employee expenses – job travel, union dues, job education, etc. You **Must** attach Form 2106 or 2106-EZ if required (See instructions.) ►	20			
	21	Tax preparation fees	21	450.		
(See instructions for expenses to deduct here.)	22	Other expenses – investment, safe deposit box, etc. List type and amount ►	22			
	23	Add lines 20 through 22	23	450.		
	24	Enter amount from Form 1040, line 33 ..... 24 77,410.				
	25	Multiply line 24 above by 2% (.02)	25	1,548.		
	26	Subtract line 25 from line 23. If line 25 is more than line 23, enter -0-			26	0.
Other Miscellaneous Deductions	27	Other – from list in the instructions. List type and amount ►			27	
Total Itemized Deductions	28	Is Form 1040, line 33, over 121,200 (over 60,600 if married filing separately)? **No.** Your deduction is not limited. Add the amounts in the far right column for lines 4 through 27. Also, enter on Form 1040, line 35, the **larger** of this amount or your standard deduction. **Yes.** Your deduction may be limited. See instructions for the amount to enter.			► 28	14,900.

Name(s) Shown on Form 1040. Do Not Enter Name and Social Security Number if Shown on Schedule A.	**Your Social Security Number**
Larry & Pat Graham	234-87-5643

Schedule B – Interest and Dividend Income

08

Part I Interest Income

(See instructions.)

Note: If you received a Form 1099-INT, Form 1099-OID, or substitute statement from a brokerage firm, list the firm's name as the payer and enter the total interest shown on that form.

Note: *If you had over 400 in taxable interest income, you must also complete Part III.*

			Amount
1	List name of payer. If any interest is from a seller-financed mortgage and the buyer used the property as a personal residence, see the instructions and list this interest first. Also, show that buyer's social security number and address ►	1	
	Bank of Wisconsin		455.00
	State of Wisconsin		250.00
	Subtotal		705.00
	Tax-Exempt Interest		-250.00
2	Add the amounts on line 1	2	455.00
3	Excludable interest on series EE U.S. savings bonds issued after 1989 from Form 8815, line 14. You **must** attach Form 8815 to Form 1040	3	
4	Subtract line 3 from line 2. Enter the result here and on Form 1040, line 8a ►	4	455.00

Part II Dividend Income

(See instructions.)

Note: If you received a Form 1099-DIV, or substitute statement from a brokerage firm, list the firm's name as the payer and enter the total dividends shown on that form.

Note: *If you had over 400 in gross dividends and/or other distributions on stock, you must also complete Part III.*

					Amount
5	List name of payer. Include gross dividends and/or other distributions on stock here. Any capital gain distributions and nontaxable distributions will be deducted on lines 7 and 8 ►			5	
	RayOVac Batteries				345.00
	Wisconsin Cheese Company				125.00
6	Add the amounts on line 5			6	470.00
7	Capital gain distributions. Enter here and on Schedule D	7			
8	Nontaxable distributions. (See the instructions for Form 1040, line 9.)	8			
9	Add lines 7 and 8			9	
10	Subtract line 9 from line 6. Enter the result here and on Form 1040, line 9 ►			10	470.00

Part III Foreign Accounts and Trusts

(See instructions.)

	You must complete this part if you **(a)** had over 400 of interest or dividends; **(b)** had a foreign account; or **(c)** received a distribution from, or were a grantor of, or a transferor to, a foreign trust.	**Yes**	**No**
11a	At any time during 1997, did you have an interest in or a signature or other authority over a financial account in a foreign country, such as a bank account, securities account, or other financial account? See instructions for exceptions and filing requirements for Form TD F 90-22.1		X
b	If 'yes,' enter the name of the foreign country ►		
12	During 1997, did you receive a distribution from, or were you the grantor of, or transferor to, a foreign trust? If 'yes,' you may have to file Form 3520 or 926. See instructions		X

Schedule D
(Form 1040)

Department of the Treasury
Internal Revenue Service

Capital Gains and Losses

► Attach to Form 1040. ► See instructions for Schedule D (Form 1040).
► Use Schedule D-1 for more space to list transactions for lines 1 and 8.

OMB No. 1545-0074
1997
12

Name(s) Shown on Form 1040: Larry & Pat Graham

Your Social Security Number: 234-87-5643

Part I — Short-Term Capital Gains and Losses — Assets Held One Year or Less

	(a) Description of property (Example: 100 shares 'XYZ' Co)	(b) Date acquired (Mo, day, yr)	(c) Date sold (Mo, day, yr)	(d) Sales price	(e) Cost or other basis	(f) GAIN or (LOSS) FOR ENTIRE YEAR. Subtract (e) from (d)
1	100 shs. Apple Computer	04/10/97	08/22/97	1,200.00	1,300.00	-100.00
2	Enter your short-term totals, if any, from Schedule D-1, line 2		2			
3	**Total short-term sales price amounts.** Add column (d) of lines 1 and 2		3	1,200.00		
4	Short-term gain from Forms 2119 and 6252, and short-term gain or (loss) from Forms 4684, 6781, and 8824				4	
5	Net short-term gain or (loss) from partnerships, S corporations, estates, and trusts from Schedule(s) K-1				5	
6	Short-term capital loss carryover. Enter the amount, if any, from line 9 of your 1996 Capital Loss Carryover Worksheet				6	
7	**Net short-term capital gain or (loss).** Combine lines 1 through 6 in column (f) ►				7	-100.

Part II — Long-Term Capital Gains and Losses — Assets Held More Than One Year

	(a) Description of property (Example: 100 shares 'XYZ' Co)	(b) Date acquired (Mo, day, yr)	(c) Date sold (Mo, day, yr)	(d) Sales price	(e) Cost or other basis	(f) GAIN or (LOSS) FOR ENTIRE YEAR. Subtract (e) from (d)	(g) 28% RATE GAIN or (LOSS) * (see instructions)
8	500 shs. Sony	03/05/87	08/22/97	30,000.00	22,500.00	7,500.00	
9	Enter your long-term totals, if any, from Schedule D-1, line 9		9				
10	**Total long-term sales price amounts.** Add column (d) of lines 8 and 9		10	30,000.00			
11	Gain from Form 4797, Part I; long-term gain from Forms 2119, 2439, and 6252; and long-term gain or (loss) from Forms 4684, 6781, and 8824				11		
12	Net long-term gain or (loss) from partnerships, S corporations, estates, and trusts from Schedule(s) K-1				12		
13	Capital gain distributions				13		
14	Long-term capital loss carryover. Enter in both columns (f) and (g) the amount, if any, from line 14 of your 1996 Capital Loss Carryover Worksheet				14		
15	Combine lines 8 through 14 in column (g)				15		
16	**Net long-term capital gain or (loss).** Combine lines 8 through 14 in column (f) ►				16	7,500.	

* **28% Rate Gain or Loss** includes all gains and losses in Part II, column (f) from sales, exchanges, or conversions (including installment payments received) **either:**
- **Before** May 7, 1997, **or**
- **After** July 28, 1997, for assets held more than 1 year but **not** more than 18 months.

It also includes **All** 'collectibles gains and losses' (as defined in the instructions).

BAA For Paperwork Reduction Act Notice, see Form 1040 instructions.

Part III Summary of Parts I and II

17	Combine lines 7 and 16. If a loss, go to line 18. If a gain, enter the gain on Form 1040, line 13			17	7,400.
	Next: Complete Form 1040 through line 38. Then, go to **Part IV** to figure **your** tax if: • Both lines 16 and 17 are gains, **and**, • Form 1040, line 38, is more than zero.				
18	If line 17 is a loss, enter here and as a (loss) on Form 1040, line 13, the **smaller** of these losses: • The loss on line 17; **or** • (3,000) or, if married filing separately, (1,500)			18	
	Next: Complete Form 1040 through line 36. Then, complete the **Capital Loss Carryover Worksheet** if: • The loss on line 17 exceeds the loss on line 18, **or** • Form 1040, line 36, is a loss.				

Part IV Tax Computation Using Maximum Capital Gains Rates

19	Enter your taxable income from Form 1040, line 38			19	51,910.
20	Enter the **smaller** of line 16 or line 17	20	7,400.		
21	If you are filing Form 4952, enter the amount from Form 4952, line 4e	21			
22	Subtract line 21 from line 20. If zero or less, enter -0-	22	7,400.		
23	Combine lines 7 and 15. If zero or less, enter -0-	23	0.		
24	Enter the **smaller** of line 15 or line 23, but not less than zero	24	0.		
25	Enter your unrecaptured section 1250 gain, if any (see instructions)	25	0.		
26	Add lines 24 and 25	26	0.		
27	Subtract line 26 from line 22. If zero or less, enter -0-			27	7,400.
28	Subtract line 27 from line 19. If zero or less, enter -0-			28	44,510.
29	Enter the **smaller** of line 19 or 41,200 (24,650 if single; 20,600 if married filing separately; 33,050 if head of household)			29	41,200.
30	Enter the **smaller** of line 28 or line 29			30	41,200.
31	Subtract line 22 from line 19. If zero or less, enter -0-			31	44,510.
32	Enter the **larger** of line 30 or line 31			32	44,510.
33	Figure the tax on the amount on line 32. Use the Tax Table or Tax Rate Schedules, whichever applies ►			33	7,111.
34	Enter the amount from line 29			34	41,200.
35	Enter the amount from line 28			35	44,510.
36	Subtract line 35 from line 34. If zero or less, enter -0-			36	0.
37	Multiply line 36 by 10% (.10) ►			37	0.
38	Enter the **smaller** of line 19 or line 27			38	7,400.
39	Enter the amount from line 36			39	0.
40	Subtract line 39 from line 38. If zero or less, enter -0-			40	7,400.
41	Multiply line 40 by 20% (.20) ►			41	1,480.
42	Enter the **smaller** of line 22 or line 25			42	0.
43	Add lines 22 and 32	43	51,910.		
44	Enter the amount from line 19	44	51,910.		
45	Subtract line 44 from line 43. If zero or less, enter -0-			45	0.
46	Subtract line 45 from line 42. If zero or less, enter -0-			46	0.
47	Multiply line 46 by 25% (.25) ►			47	0.
48	Enter the amount from line 19			48	51,910.
49	Add lines 32, 36, 40, and 46			49	51,910.
50	Subtract line 49 from line 48			50	0.
51	Multiply line 50 by 28% (.28) ►			51	0.
52	Add lines 33, 37, 41, 47, and 51			52	8,591.
53	Figure the tax on the amount on line 19. Use the Tax Table or Tax Rate Schedules, whichever applies			53	9,183.
54	**Tax.** Enter the **smaller** of line 52 or line 53 here and on Form 1040, line 39 ►			54	8,591.

Form **2441** | Department of the Treasury Internal Revenue Service (99)

Child and Dependent Care Expenses

▸ Attach to Form 1040.
▸ See separate instructions.

OMB No. 1545-0068
1997
21

Name(s) Shown on Form 1040: Larry & Pat Graham | Your Social Security Number: 234-87-5643

Before you begin, you need to understand the following terms. See **Definitions** in the instructions.

- **Dependent Care Benefits**
- **Qualifying Person(s)**
- **Qualified Expenses**
- **Earned Income**

Part I **Persons or Organizations Who Provided the Care** — You **must** complete this part.
(If you need more space, use the bottom of page 2.)

1 (a) Care provider's name	(b) Address (no., street, apt no., city, state, and ZIP code)	(c) Identifying number (SSN or EIN)	(d) Amount paid (see instructions)
Madison Care	1299 Regent St. Madison, WI 53706	66-2345677	2,600.00

Did you receive **dependent care benefits?** — **No** ⟶ Complete only Part II below. **Yes** ⟶ Complete Part III on page 2 next.

Caution: *If the care was provided in your home, you may owe employment taxes. See the instructions for Form 1040, line 52.*

Part II **Credit for Child and Dependent Care Expenses**

2 Information about your **qualifying person(s).** If you have more than two qualifying persons, see the instructions.

(a) Qualifying person's name — First	Last	(b) Qualifying person's social security number	(c) Qualified expenses you incurred and paid in 1997 for the person listed in column (a)
Larry	Graham Jr.	233-11-2311	1,300.
Michelle	Graham	233-44-5566	1,300.

		Line	Amount
3	Add the amounts in column (c) of line 2. **Do not** enter more than 2,400 for one qualifying person or 4,800 for two or more persons. If you completed Part III, enter the amount from line 24	3	2,600.
4	Enter **your earned income**	4	35,000.
5	If married filing a joint return, enter **your spouse's** earned income (If student or disabled, see the instructions); **all others**, enter the amount from line 4	5	34,000.
6	Enter the **smallest** of line 3, 4, or 5	6	2,600.
7	Enter the amount from Form 1040, line 33 — 7: 77,410.		
8	Enter on line 8 the decimal amount shown below that applies to the amount on line 7	8	X 0.20

If line 7 is – Over	But not over	Decimal amount is	If line 7 is – Over	But not over	Decimal amount is
0	10,000	.30	20,000	22,000	.24
10,000	12,000	.29	22,000	24,000	.23
12,000	14,000	.28	24,000	26,000	.22
14,000	16,000	.27	26,000	28,000	.21
16,000	18,000	.26	28,000	No limit	.20
18,000	20,000	.25			

		Line	Amount
9	Multiply **line 6** by the decimal amount on line 8. Enter the result. Then, see the instructions for the amount of credit to enter on Form 1040, line 40	9	520.

PROBLEM 3 Carl and Christie Clennick

Objective: Sample problem and solution. Self-employed taxpayer with depreciation and Section 179 deduction.

Carl and Christie Clennick, both age 36, are married and live at 1080 Schelter Road, Lincolnshire, IL 60197. Carl, Social Security number 287-65-4321, is a self-employed carpenter. Christie is a teacher at Lincolnshire High School. She reports the following W-2 information:

Home Address	1080 Schelter Road, Lincolnshire, IL 60197
Telephone number	217-555-5555
Social security number	345-67-8910
Employer	Lincolnshire School District, 23 Court House Road, Lincolnshire, ILL 60191, employer number 33-8765432
Wages	$ 23,000
Federal income taxes W/H	3,600
State income taxes W/H	1,080
Social security taxes	1,426
Medicare taxes	333

The Clennicks have two dependent sons - Cleveland (age 8) and Mayo (age 5). The children's Social Security numbers are 123-45-6789 and 234-56-7890, respectively. The Clennicks have presented you with the following tax information for the current year.

1. The Clennicks both support the President Election Campaign Fund.

2. The Clennicks received interest of $550 from First National Bank of Lincolnshire. They also received dividends of $525 from General Products Corporation and $125 from Acme Supplies, Inc. The Clennicks do not have an interest in any foreign accounts.

3. For the last two years, Carl was employed as a carpenter by Lincolnshire Contractors, Inc. On January 3 of the current tax year, he started his own business - Clennick Carpenter Service, 2125 Main Street, Lincolnshire, IL, 60197, employer identification number 22-1234567. He uses the cash method of reporting.

   Carl continued to use the tools and equipment (all fully depreciated) he owned and used while employed by Lincolnshire Contractors. In addition, he purchased a new light-duty pick-up truck for $16,000 on January 5. He drove the truck 20,000 miles during the year (8,000 for personal use and 12,000 for business). He did not use the truck for any other purposes, and no one else used it. He elected to compute the cost recovery allowance for the truck using prescribed statutory percentages and he chose not to expense the truck under Section 179. Also, Carl purchased some new tools on February 1 that cost $1,200. Carl wants to expense these tools under section 179. Carl's other income and expense items relating to his business are summarized below:

Total income	$	56,000
Expenses:		
Advertising		1,600
Bank service charges		1,100
Truck operating expenses		2,500
Insurance		1,200
Legal and professional services		1,400
Supplies		1,900
Utilities and telephone		1,300

4. Christie attended a three-day teacher's convention in New York and incurred $600 of unreimbursed expenses for airfare and lodging.

5. Carl and Christie each made a contribution of $2,000 to separate Individual Retirement Accounts (i.e. a total contribution of $4,000 for the two of them.) In addition Christie's employer contributed $2,400 to the Illinois State Retirement Fund on her behalf. The state retirement fund is a qualified retirement plan.

6. The Clennicks incurred the following expenses during the current year:

a.	Estimated payments on state income tax (Paid quarterly; last payment December 31, 1997)	$	740
b.	Additional payment of 1996 state income tax (Paid April, 1997)		420
c.	Real estate taxes on personal residence		650
d.	Home mortgage interest		980
e.	Credit card interest		300
f.	Charitable contributions (cash) to State U		800
g.	Professional dues (Christie)		940

7. The Clennicks paid an unrelated child care service, Child Care Company, 23 Main Street, Douglas, IL 60001, $350 per month during the year. The services were provided in the Clennick's home. Child Care's EIN is 66-7788990.

8. The Clennicks made total estimated Federal tax payments of $9,200, consisting of four $2,300 payments that were made on April 15, June 15 and September 15, 1997 and January 15, 1998.

REQUIRED: Use TurboTax to prepare and print the Federal income tax return.

PROBLEM 4 Lynn and Heather O'Keefe

Objective: Upper income taxpayer, entertainment expenses, distribution from an IRA, dependent elderly parent, and home business tax problems.

Lynn O'Keefe, age 53, is president of O'Keefes Furniture Store. He reports the following W-2 information:

Home Address	46 Germantown Rd., Chattanooga, TN 37411
Telephone	615-555-5555
Social security number	524-67-2343
Employer	O'Keefes Furniture store, 1201 Hamilton Ave., Chattanooga, TN 37401, employer number 64-1453236.
Wages	$98,000
Federal income taxes W/H	$24,640
Social security taxes	$ 3,887
Medicare taxes	$ 1,421

Heather O'Keefe, age 50, social security number 446-18-3904, works at home as a housewife.

Both Lynn and Heather want $3 of their taxes to go the to Presidential Election Campaign Fund. The O'Keefe children are grown. However, Heather's mother, Molly Shoulders, lives with them. Molly received social security of $5,400, and interest income of $5,000 during the year. She has no other income.

In addition to the income above, Lynn and Heather incurred the following tax transactions during the year:

1. Interest income from the Hamilton National Bank, $680.

2. Lynn received a pre-mature distribution from an IRA account of $28,500, which he used to purchase a new car.

3. The O'Keefes have no interest in any foreign accounts or trusts.

4. Lynn purchased 10,000 shares of Bassett Inc. stock on April 22, 1981 for $120,000. He sold the stock on August 12, 1997 for $91,200.

5. To promote the family business, Lynn and Heather give a large party at Christmas time for all their best customers. The party cost $2,300.

6. During the year, Lynn drove his personal automobile 30,000 miles including 3,000 miles to and from work, and 2,000 round and about town. The other 25,000 miles were related to business trips (to buy furniture). The company reimbursed him at a rate of 20 cents per mile ($5,000) for those business trips. In addition, Lynn spent $2,500 for

meals and $4,800 for lodging while on the business trips. The cost of meals was not reimbursed by his company because he forgot to file for reimbursement. If he had filed a reimbursement request, the company would have paid for the meals. The lodging was fully reimbursed by the company.

7. Heather has a good reputation as a home decorator. She writes articles and gives seminars around Chattanooga. The amount of business has been small, so she has not applied for a business license. However, she did receive the following for some of her work.

   a. Article in *Southern Living*, $250.
   b. Seminar on Medical Office decor for Erlanger Hospital, $75.
   c. "Gift" for decorating Dr. Barber's office, $100.
   d. "Gift" for doing flower arrangements at a friend's wedding, $20.
   e. McCallie Schools, for seminar on keeping rooms clean, $65.

   Note: An Itemize statement may be required to report all of these miscellaneous income items.

   To allow her to prepare outlines and hand out materials for these seminars and to write her articles, Heather spent $2,200 to purchase a personal computer and $1,500 to purchase a nice laser printer. The PC and printer were used 80% of the time to further her career as a home decorator. The balance, 20%, was used for personal letters and using Quicken to keep her check book accurate.

8. Potential itemized deductions included the following:
   a. Medical expenses included health insurance of $2,500; medical expenses paid for Molly in excess of Medicare, $12,000; Heather's eyeglasses $500.
   b. Real estate taxes, $1,000.
   c. Sales taxes on purchases, $1,520.
   d. Home mortgage interest paid to bank, $4,400.
   e. Interest on bank credit cards, $1,050.
   f. Cash contributions to their church, $5,500.
   g. Fee for preparation of personal income tax return, $600.

REQUIRED: Complete the federal income tax return.

PROBLEM 5 Crystal Ball

Objective: Single professional with IRA, investment income, moving expense and gross income problems.

Crystal Ball, age 36, is single and has no dependents. She is employed by Banker Corporation as an account manager. She reports the following W-2 information:

Home Address	2323 Westview Street, Chicago, IL 60680.
Social security number	366-55-2222
Employer	Banker Corporation, 45 Michigan Ave., Chicago, IL 60611, employer number 35-9765432
Wages	$63,000
Federal income taxes W/H	$15,000
State income taxes W/H	$ 2,500
Social security taxes	$ 3,887
Medicare taxes	$ 899

From Crystal's prior year tax return, you note that a federal tax refund of $325 was to be applied to current year federal taxes. You further note that she used the standard deduction for both federal and state returns last year. Lastly, you note that she received a state income tax refund of $24 during the current tax year (1997) from her prior year state return (1996). Also, you absolutely lastly note that Crystal does not have a telephone -- she hates to get calls at home.

Crystal earned interest of $1,850 from Second National Bank of Chicago. Crystal, as a new employee at Banker Corporation, is not eligible for any qualified pension plan. Accordingly, she contributed $2,000 to a new 1997 Individual Retirement Account in February, 1998. In addition, on March 7, 1997, she purchased 100 shares of Banker Corporation at a price of $86 per share. In December, 1997, she received a stock dividend of 5 shares, when the stock was valued at $90 per share. Before Crystal decided to purchase the stock she bought the Sure-fired Stock Advisor, an annual publication advising on stock trends, for $29.95.

Prior to working at Banker Corporation, Crystal worked for First Wisconsin in Milwaukee. As a part of her job offer, on January 8 of the current tax year, Banker paid Crystal $3,000 as a moving allowance. Crystal rented a truck and move herself (a distance of 120 miles,) incurring a cost of $800 for the truck rental. On January 4, 5, and 6, Crystal traveled to Chicago to look for an apartment. She stayed with friends from college. She took her friends out as payment for allowing her to stay with them. The cost of dinner *et al* was $340. She drove her own car, traveling a total of 300 miles. When Crystal mentioned these costs to her new boss, she was told that part of her moving allowance was to cover these kinds of costs -- she did not receive any more from Banker Corporation.

On January 31, 1997 Crystal received a check for $200 from Brewer Apartments in Milwaukee, in refund of her apartment deposit. In January of 1996, Crystal paid an apartment deposit to the Cubs Apartments in Chicago in the amount of $100. While deciding what to do with the refund check, Crystal noted that the distance from her old apartment in Milwaukee to her old job was 10 miles. Coincidentally, the distance from her new apartment to her new job is also 10 miles. Thus, she moved 120 miles and she is still 10 miles from work. But a lot closer to the Cubs games.

In April of the current tax year, Crystal was surprised by a visit from her old roommate from college, Sue. Even more astonishing to Crystal, Sue paid her $500, the amount plus some interest, she had loaned Sue in College. Sue determined that $50 of that amount was for interest. Crystal considered the entire amount to be repayment of a $450 loan that she had deducted five years earlier as a nonbusiness loan.
In September of the current tax year, Crystal was asked by a friend, Jon, to do some research/consulting work to advise him on the feasibility of a new business. Crystal spent three weekends in the Chicago library gathering information. She incurred $125 in photocopying bills. She also incurred $50 purchasing paper and other supplies that were consumed in the project. Jon agreed to pay her $400 for the project. After a total of 50 hours of work, Crystal delivered the report. Jon told her to forget it; he had decided to marry Gail and live on her money instead. In December, Jon sent Crystal a box of cheeses that cost him (or Gail) $50, with a note that said "Thanks for all your help." Jon sent these to all of his old friends.

Crystal elects to designate $3 of her taxes to the Presidential Election Campaign Fund. If Crystal is entitled to a refund, she would like to have it applied to her next year's Federal income tax as she did last year.

REQUIRED: Prepare Crystal's tax return.

PROBLEM 6 Vern Wilson

Objective: Wage earner return with miscellaneous income.

Vern Wilson has asked you to file his Federal income tax return. He is single, has no dependents, and is employed as an electrical engineer. He has given you the following information taken from his W-2 and other sources.

Home Address	221 Main Street, Newburyport, MA 01950.
Telephone	617-555-5555
Social security number	285-33-1543
Employer	Acme Components, Inc., 8 Henry Cove, Hedgemouth, MA 01999, employer number 44-5665432
Wages	$60,000
Federal income taxes W/H	$14,500
State income taxes W/H	$ 3,200
Social security taxes	$ 3,720
Medicare taxes	$ 870

1. He received interest of $1,200 on a savings account at Second National Bank, and received dividends of $800 on Acme Components, Inc. stock he owns. He has no interest in any other bank or trust accounts.

2. Vern won a $1,000 lottery prize in November.

3. Vern made a $2,000 contribution to his Individual Retirement Account (IRA) in December. Vern did not contribute to any other qualified plan, neither did his employer.

4. Vern received a refund of state income taxes in the amount of $245. In 1996, Vern took the standard deduction.

5. Acme Components greatly values Vern's work and tries to keep him happy at work. His boss redecorated his office spending $3,000 on furniture that Vern selected. Acme purchased a new personal computer with CD ROM drives and a sound card, costing $4,000 for Vern's use at home. Vern reports that 40 percent of its use was related to his job at Acme; the balance was personal use. Vern also was able to use the corporation's ocean front condo for three weeks during June. The fair market rental value of the condo is $1,000 per week. Jon was the only employee allowed to use the condo. The condo was used the rest of the year by customers only. The marginal cost to the corporation (utilities and cleaning) of Jon's using the condo was $150 per week. None of these amounts were included on Vern's W-2; the bookkeeper considered these items to be non-taxable.

6. Vern collects things. During the year, Vern sold some of the things that he had collected for a total of $7,500. In addition, Vern purchased several new things that cost a total of $10,000. Vern also incurred transportation costs of $1,200 going to sales where he bought some things and

sold some things. Vern does not keep any kind of inventory records. He estimates that the things he has in inventory cost about $30,000 but have a fair market value of $60,000. Vern does not have a business license, nor is his home in an area that is zoned for business. Vern stores all of his things at his home.

Vern's barber told him that he had to file a Schedule C and pay self-employment taxes because he was in the business of buying and selling things. Vern considers himself to have a hobby, albeit one that allows him to make some money. Ah, the joys of taxes.

7. Vern elects to support the Presidential Election Campaign Fund.

REQUIRED: Prepare and print Vern Wilson's federal income tax return.

PROBLEM 7 George and Martha Jefferson

Objective: Kiddy tax, property transactions, itemized deductions, scholarships

George Jefferson, age 44, attends a nearby university on a full-time basis studying accounting. His Social Security number is 387-65-4346. His wife, Martha, age 45, is currently employed full time at the local First National Bank as a branch manager. The Jeffersons have two dependent daughters, Sarah (age 14) and Emily (age 12) whose Social Security numbers are 387-65-4347 and 387-65-4348, respectively. They provide you with the following information about Martha's wages.

Home Address	123 Mountainview Lane, Monticello, Virginia 22901
Telephone	804-555-5555
Social security number	387-65-4345
Employer	First National Bank, 18 Main St., Charlottesville, VA 22916, employer number 66-5566443
Wages	$33,000
Federal income taxes W/H	$ 1,300
State income taxes W/H	$ 1,650
Social security taxes	$ 2,046
Medicare taxes	$ 478

In addition to Martha's W-2 information, the Jefferson's report the following.

1. The Jeffersons received a refund of 1996 Virginia income taxes of $45. In 1996, the Jeffersons' itemized deductions amounted to $7,498. Their 1996 taxable income was $28,000.

2. George, is in the Ph.D. program. He received a "full" scholarship of $8,000. Tuition amounted to $5,000, while books and required supplies were $800. In addition George spent $1,800 traveling ($600 for public transportation, $500 for food, and $700 for lodging) to Washington, DC to use the SEC's library, $1,000 photocopying financial statements, $1,000 to hire a statistical consultant, and $300 to hire an editor. These expenses related to George's research work for his Ph.D. dissertation.

3. During the year, Martha's parents made several cash gifts to the Jeffersons. The gifts were invested in a First National Bank money market accounts which generated $650 of interest income to George and Martha; interest income to Sarah of $4,000; and Emily received $3,500 in interest income.

4. The Jeffersons support the Presidential Election Campaign Fund.

5. During the year the following stock transactions were made:

Stock	Date Acquired	Date Sold	Sales Price	Cost
ABC Corp.	12/30/87	5/31/97	$2,400	$1,200
JUNK Corp.	9/15/96	8/25/97	2,000	8,000

6. The Jeffersons incurred the following expenses during the year:

a.	Sales tax on the purchase of a new car	$ 400
b.	Cash charitable contributions (U of Virginia)	1,000
c.	Student loan interest	2,500
d.	Interest on home mortgage	3,300
e.	Safety Deposit Box rental (for securities)	50
f.	Tax return preparation fee	400
g.	Real estate taxes	700
h.	Personal property taxes (based upon value)	250

7. During the year, the Jeffersons made a charitable contribution of XYZ stock to the University of Virginia. George had purchased the stock May 2, 1981 for $100. On April 1 of the current tax year, the *Wall Street Journal* provided a market quote indicating the value was $1,500.

8. George and Martha strongly supports the women's athletic programs at the University of Virginia. In August of the current tax year, George donated $500 to the athletic department's "CavsR'us Club." Members of this club receive two tickets for women's basketball with seats at mid-court and a preferential parking space in Lot 22. The normal price for season tickets is $50 each. Parking in Lot 22 is not otherwise available on game day.

9. To enable George to attend school, the Jeffersons hired Nanny Smith who lives at 333 Childress Lane in Monticello. Her SSN is 444-33-2222 and she was paid at a monthly rate of $350 to care for Sarah and Emily. The Jeffersons completed the appropriate wage tax forms. Their employer identification number is 23-4875789.

REQUIRED: Prepare and print the Federal income tax return for George and Martha Jefferson.

PROBLEM 8 Ronald Lump

Objective: Self-employed professional, office in home

Ronald Lump, 55, is an unmarried, self-employed medical doctor and resides at 2601 Pennsylvania Avenue, Washington D.C. 20001. His Social Security number is 387-12-3456. Ronald's wife died last year, but he continues to maintain a home for his blind 16 year-old dependent son Ronald, Jr., whose Social Security number is 387-12-3457. Ronald's telephone number is 202-555-1234.

The relevant tax information given to you includes the following:

1. Ronald uses the cash method of accounting in his business. His employer identification number is 33-1234567. Income and expenses pertaining to his business follow:

a.	Fees collected	$ 295,000
b.	Bad debt written off	2,000
c.	Legal and accounting services	2,500
d.	Qualifying business meals and entertainment	1,400
e.	Medical journals	800
f.	Office supplies	1,300
g.	Continuing education self-study courses	3,550
h.	Malpractice insurance	34,000
i.	Part-time secretary from "Kelly Girl"	10,000

2. During the year, Ronald worked at City Hospital and University Hospital, both in Bethesda, Maryland. While he spent 30 to 35 hours per week working at the hospitals, Ronald was not provided with an office at either hospital.

   Instead, Ronald used a bedroom in his house as his office, where he kept a computer, an answering machine, a copier, telephone, patient records, and medical books and journals. From the office, Ronald contacted other doctors and patients by phone. In addition, he often called hospitals to arrange admission for his own patients. He did all necessary to bill his patients in this office. He also spent time in his office reading medical books and journals, and preparing for patients; however, Ronald did not see any patients at his office. On average, Ronald spent 16 hours per week working in his home office during this year. Ronald did not use the office for any non-business purposes. His part-time secretary also worked in the home office.

Ronald has the following expenses relevant to determining a home office expense deduction:

a. The bedroom office represented approximately 20% of the total square footage of his house.
b. Total interest expense paid on his home mortgage was $17,000.
c. Ronald's annual utility bills for the residence were $2,800.
d. Property taxes on the house amounted to $2,100 for the year.
e. Ronald paid $210,000 for the house when he purchased it on January 1 of this year.
f. Ronald has a second telephone line that can only be answered in his office. The cost of this business phone was $480 for the year.

3. In March, Ronald purchased office furniture costing $8,000. Ronald wishes to maximize any deduction relating to this furniture that is available to him this year.

4. Ronald made timely estimated Federal income tax payments of $80,000 ($20,000 each quarter) during the year; the fourth quarter payment was made on January 15, 1998. He also made estimated income tax payments for a total of $3,200 to the Maryland and the District's Commissioners of Revenue. Ronald made the last quarter's payment to both jurisdictions on December 31, 1997. He wanted that tax deduction. Ronald made an additional payment of $345 when he filed his 1996 D.C. income tax return in April, 1997. Ronald paid $125 in additional income taxes for 1996 to Maryland when he filed in April, 1997.

5. Ronald received $1,000 in dividends on savings held in a D.C. Savings Bank time deposit. In addition, he received a $600 dividend payment from his mutual life insurance company on a policy that he owns on his life. He paid premiums on the policy of $2,500 during the year.

6. Ronald received the final settlement on the life insurance policy held on the life of Mrs. Lump. He received a lump-sum of $100,000, plus the first payment of $5,500, a life-time annuity. The insurance company reported that $1,500 of this amount was interest.

7. Ronald's other tax-related transactions were:

a. Doctor fees incurred for Ronald, Jr., $5,000
b. Real estate taxes on land held as an investment in Haiti, $500
c. Ronald elects to support the Presidential Election Campaign Fund.

REQUIRED: Prepare and print Ronald Lump's Federal income tax return.

PROBLEM 9 John and Jane Elder

Objective: Semi-retired wages, investment income, retirement income

John and Jane Elder, who are both semi-retired, live at 1040 Lakeview Drive, Orlando, Florida 32801. Their telephone number is 904-555-4444. John, who is 65, enjoys working part-time in the clubhouse at the Gator Golf Club, while Jane, who is 66 and legally blind, works at a local music store, Thomas Piano Company, as a piano tuner. John's and Jane's Social Security numbers are 154-32-1234 and 265-43-2123, respectively. The information presented relates to their activities during the current tax year.

1. From John's $15,000 salary earned at the Gator Golf Club, federal income taxes withheld were $1,200, Social Security taxes withheld were $930, and Medicare taxes withheld were $218.

2. Jane's earnings totaled $13,000; withholding for federal income tax was $540; for Social security, $806; and for Medicare tax, $188.

3. Other items of income received during the year included:

   a. John's pension from his former employer was $4,800. All contributions to the pension fund were provided by Alcoa, his former employer.
   b. Interest Income:
      i. Best Money Market Fund, $850
      ii. First Orlando Bank, $2,450
      iii. Interest on a City of Miami general obligation bond, $600
      iv. The Elders have no accounts in foreign banks.

4. Other Income:

   a. Dividends from Security Corporation stock, $3,000
   b. Taxable pension proceeds from Security Corporation, $5,000
   c. Jane received an annuity of $300 per month from the Rock Insurance Company. The proceeds were paid in accordance with a single premium annuity policy Jane had purchased 30 years ago for $12,000. 1997 is the second full year of the 10-year term certain annuity policy.

5. As a result of a hurricane during September, the Elders' Volvo station wagon was totally destroyed. Its value at the time of destruction was $15,000, while its original cost was $22,000 when purchased on October 1, 1993. Unfortunately, the auto was not insured; John forgot to pay the bill.

6. Because of circulatory problems diagnosed during a routine physical examination, Jane's physician recommended that she begin a daily swimming routine. There are no pools available to the Elders. Consequently, the Elders had a swimming pool constructed in their backyard. While the cost of the pool was $15,000, it only increased the value of the home by $5,000.

7. Routine uninsured medical expenses included:

a.	Doctors	$500
b.	Prescription medicines	600
c.	Over-the-counter medications	150
d.	Medicare, part B	500

8. Other expenditures made during the year include:

a.	Gift to their son	$10,000
b.	Cash charitable contribution	4,500
c.	Tax return preparation fee	300

9. In the event a tax refund is due, the Elders would like one-half of it credited to their tax liability for next tax year. They both fully support the Presidential Election Campaign Fund.

REQUIRED: Prepare and print the Elders' Federal income tax return.

PROBLEM 10 Nancy and Steve Ferguson

Objective: Stock transactions, itemized deductions, tax refund

Nancy and Steve Ferguson, both 36, are married and live at 777 Millbrook Court, Charlotte, North Carolina 28203. Their telephone number is 704-444-5555. Nancy's Social Security number is 223-34-4556 and Steve's Social Security number is 277-88-9900. They fully support the Presidential Election Campaign Fund.

1. Nancy teaches home economics at Charlotte High School and earns an annual salary of $25,000. Federal income taxes withheld were $3,000, Social Security taxes withheld were $1,550, and Medicare taxes withheld were $362. State income taxes withheld were $1,500.

2. Steve was employed at Millbrook Lumber Co., a lumber yard, as an inventory specialist. His W-2 showed a salary for the year of $28,000. From his earnings, Federal income taxes withheld were $3,500, Social Security taxes withheld were $1,736, and Medicare taxes withheld were $406. State income taxes withheld were $1,680.

3. During the year, the Fergusons received a $600 refund because of an overpayment of their previous year's North Carolina income tax liability. Last year they itemized their deductions on their federal income tax return. (In 1996, Schedule A, Line 26 was $8,660 and taxable income was $40,700.)

4. During the year the following transactions were executed:

Item	Date Acquired	Date Sold	Sales Price	Cost
Personal automobile	3/30/85	9/30/97	$ 3,000	$10,000
XYZ Stock	10/20/95	7/ 3/97	$23,000	$22,500
CDE Stock	1/ 3/80	12/31/97	$ 9,000	$ 6,000
FGH Stock	9/30/97	11/28/97	$ 1,000	$ 3,000

5. On December 29, 1997, Nancy and Steve sold 1,000 shares of MNO Corp. stock to Nancy's brother. The sales price was $5,000. The MNO stock was originally purchased by the Fergusons for $7,500 on October 26, 1984. Because of their hope that the stock would rebound, Nancy repurchased the stock from her brother for $5,100 on January 8, 1997.

6. Other tax related expenditures include the following:

   a. Employee expenses for lodging incurred by Steve on a business trip -- reimbursed and included in Steve's W-2, $600
   b. Contribution -- First Reformed Church, $1,500
   c. Credit card and automobile loan interest, $600
   d. Mortgage interest on personal residence, $4,000
   e. Interest paid on home equity loan totaled $3,500
   f. Property taxes on home, $1,780

REQUIRED: Prepare and print Nancy and Steve's Federal income tax return.

PROBLEM 11 Dick Craig

Objective: High income, divorced, sale of home, stock option

Dick Craig, 47, is the vice-president of Marketing for the St. Louis Beverage Company, One Main Street, St. Louis. He lives at 5414 Presidential Lane, St. Charles, Missouri 63301, and his telephone number is 314-555-5555. Dick's Social Security number is 477-22-5900. The information presented relates to his activities in 1996.

1. Dick's salary was $175,000. Federal income taxes withheld were $45,000, state income taxes were $10,800, Social security taxes were $3,887, and Medicare taxes were $1,958.

2. Interest income from Bank of St. Charles, $2,000

3. Dividends on St. Louis Beverage stock, $12,000

4. In 1995, Dick and his wife Esther were divorced. The divorce decree awarded custody of their son, Bob, to Esther and provides that Esther is to receive $400 per month for child support. The decree further stipulates that Dick was to pay $140,000 of alimony in 1995, $80,000 of alimony in 1996, and $4,000 per month as alimony for 1997 and later years. Dick paid the alimony and child support as required by the divorce decree.

5. The divorce decree also required that Dick and Esther's home be sold and the proceeds divided equally between them. Dick handled the sale. On January 10 of the current tax year, the house was sold for $250,000. The joint basis in the house was $180,000. Real estate commissions of $13,500 were paid on the sale. The existing mortgage on the house had a balance of $120,000, which Dick paid off. The balance of the proceeds was distributed equally to Dick and Esther on January 15.

6. On March 15, Dick purchased his current home. The cost was $150,000. Dick paid $15,000 down and obtained a mortgage of $135,000 from the Bank of St. Charles. He was able to obtain an interest rate on the mortgage of 6% by paying 1 point ($1,350), which is the standard practice in the area. During the current tax year, Dick paid $6,100 interest on the mortgage in addition to the 1 point.

7. On July 1, as a result of his annual performance evaluation, Dick was granted an option to purchase 10,000 shares of St. Louis Beverage stock for $50 per share, the then market value. Dick agreed to purchase the shares. He borrowed the entire amount from the St. Charles Bank. (His brother is president of the bank.) During the remainder of the year, he paid $20,000 in interest on the loan.

8. Dick fully supports the Presidential Election Campaign Fund. In addition, Dick contributed $500 to the Committee to Reelect Senator Scandal.

9. Dick received a refund of state income taxes in the amount of $386. On his last year's tax return, Dick had itemized deductions of $15,000 and taxable income of $105,000.

10. Additional expenditures incurred during the current year were:

    a. Cash contribution to U of Missouri, $1,500
    b. Property taxes on his home, $3,500
    c. Interest on car loan, $2,800

11. Dick has no interest in any foreign accounts.

REQUIRED: Prepare and print Dick's Federal income tax return.

PROBLEM 12 Louise and Ernie Hansen

Objective: High income, self-employed taxpayer with an AMT problem

Louise and Ernie Hansen left the hassles of big city life to move to the small town that the world has forgotten and that has no telephones anywhere in town. They currently live at 52 Lake Rd., Lake Wobegon, Minnesota 55457. Louise's Social Security number is 257-15-1122 and Ernie's is 075-22-1993. Ernie is the author of a series of self-improvement books. His latest is *How to better organize your office*. His publisher is sure it will be a best seller. Louise and Ernie report the following potentially useful information for their current year tax computation.

1. Ernie received royalties of $5,400 this year -- not a good year for self-improvement books.

2. Ernie received $75,000 from Minnesota Investment Fund, a specialized mutual fund that invests only in State of Minnesota municipal bonds. The distribution was entirely from interest. The fund did not sell any of its bonds during the year.

3. Louise inherited $200,000 cash from her father's estate. She used part of the funds to fix up the house and put the remainder in certificates of deposit at the Bank of Lake Wobegon. She received interest income of $5,600.

4. In February, Ernie and Louise finally settled a long tax dispute with the State of New York. As a result, Ernie paid $39,000 in back taxes and $5,000 in interest. In addition, he had to pay New York $4,000 in penalties.

5. March 19 was Louise's lucky day. She won the Lake Wobegon lottery. As a result she received the first of twenty $75,000 annual payments. State taxes withheld amounted to $6,000. Federal income taxes of $21,000 were withheld. No Social Security or Medicare taxes were withheld.

6. On December 1, Ernie cashed some of Louise's CDs and borrowed more to purchased a small, newly constructed shopping center in Lake Wobegon. He got it at a good price. The cost of the building was $550,000 and the land cost $75,000. Ernie decided to have the parking lot paved, at a cost of $50,000. Interest on the mortgage for the part year was $8,500. He held the shopping center in his own name. While he advertised for tenants in December, the first tenant did not move in until January 2, 1998; thus, he had no income from the property during the current tax year (1997).

7. The Hansens fully support the Presidential Election Campaign Fund.

8. Additional expenditures incurred during the current year were:

   a. Cash contribution to St. Cloud State University, $3,500
   b. Property taxes on their home, $2,500
   c. Interest on car loan, $1,800

9. It was a balmy day in May, three years ago, when the Hansens moved to Lake Wobegon. Among the several things they forgot, was to begin paying estimated taxes. They have been consistent ever since. Thus, no estimated taxes were paid for the current year's taxes.

10. Concerned about his retirement years, Ernie decided to invest for the future. Accordingly, in June, he opened an IRA account at the local office of Oats Last, an investment brokerage firm. He contributed $2,000 to his account and $2,000 to an account for Louise. The funds were invested in equity stocks. At the end of the year, Ernie's account was valued at $1,900; Louise's was valued at $2,300. He should have invested in the same stocks as Louise.

REQUIRED: Prepare and print the Hansen's Federal income tax return.

PROBLEM 13 Bill and June Barber

Objective: Investment activities

Bill and June Barber live in a small town, Leroy, North Dakota. However, they are able to engage in a variety of investment activities from their town. They live at 1 Archer Lane, Leroy, ND 58252. Their telephone number is 701-555-5555. Bill's Social Security number is 254-35-7622 and June's is 475-32-1286. The tax events of 1996 for Bill and June are listed below.

1. Bill received interest from the Bank of Leroy, of $12,400.

2. June received the following dividends:

    a. General Motors, $23,890
    b. General Electric, $2,600
    c. General Dynamics, $3,500
    d. General Tire Company, $2,300
    e. General Consulting Service, Inc., $345

3. Bill purchased a tract of Texas farm land 30 years ago for $40,000. On January 5, it was worth $60,000. He exchanged it for farm land outside of Leroy (FMV $58,000). Later, on August 4, Bill sold one fourth of his Leroy land for $16,000, paying a sales commission of $1,600.

4. Bill is a 50% owner in a limited partnership that owns a variety of real estate across the country. In prior years, the partnership reported several losses. As a result of the past losses, Bill has a passive activity loss carryover of $13,000. On August 4, Bill sold his entire interest in the partnership for $340,000. At the time of sale, his basis was $334,000. The partnership reported no income or loss for the current tax year.

5. The Barbers paid estimated federal income taxes of $1,000 per quarter. In addition, they paid estimated state income taxes of $200 per quarter. Thinking ahead, the Barbers paid their fourth quarter payments in December of the current tax year.

6. Ten years ago, Bill paid $240,000 for a tract of land he is holding as an investment outside of Dallas, Texas. The purchase price was comprised of $40,000 cash and a 20-year mortgage for $200,000 with a 12% rate. In October of this year, Bill was able to refinance the mortgage obtaining a new rate of 7%, and a new term of 10 years. To refinance the mortgage, he had to pay $1,000 in closing costs plus 1 point. These were the normal fees in the area. The total amount paid as interest (excluding the point) for the year was $18,000.

7. The Barbers fully support the Presidential Election Campaign Fund.

8. Additional expenditures incurred during the current year were:

   a. Cash contribution to University of Tennessee, $2,400
   b. Bank mortgage interest on their home, $6,890
   c. Property taxes on their home, $1,200
   d. Interest on car loan, $800

REQUIRED: Prepare and print the Barbers' Federal income tax return.

PROBLEM 14 Roger and Barbara Holly

Objective: Small business with like-kind exchanges

Roger Holly, social security number 423-98-9876, operates an electrical contractor company at 111 French Avenue, Fries, Virginia 243301. The company has been expanding each year for the past several years. Currently, the company has five employees. Barbara Holly works in her home as a homemaker and as a part-time bookkeeper for the company.

Barbara's social security number is 422-45-6912 and they live on Route 3, Box 45, Fries, VA 24330. Their telephone number is 540-555-5454. They have two children. Bill is ten and his social security number is 456-23-7865. Matthew is seven and his SSN is 458-54-2389. Neither child had any income.

Both Roger and Barbara support the Presidential Election Campaign Fund.

Information about the business and their other tax transactions is listed below:

1. Estimated federal income tax paid for the current tax year are $12,000; estimated state income tax paid during the current tax year are $2,500. In addition, they paid additional state income taxes relating to the previous year's income of $125 in April of the current tax year.

2. Interest income from the Bank of Fries, $655

3. Rental income from a small four unit apartment house that Barbara owns was $17,400. Barbara purchased the apartment house on February 4 for $145,000 and immediately begin renting the apartments. The mortgage interest on the apartments for the current year is $13,500; insurance is $500; and property taxes are $650. Roger did all the repairs at no cost to Barbara. (The cost of materials for the repairs ($125) was included in the expenses of Roger's business.)

4. The Hollys have no interest in any foreign accounts or trusts.

5. Roger trades trucks as often as he can afford to in order to minimize repair costs. On June 5, he was able to trade two trucks for new trucks. The new trucks (trucks 5 and 6) cost him a total of $10,000 in addition to the trade-in. The fair market value of the trucks (5 and 6) are $23,000 in total. The trucks that were traded-in (trucks 3 and 4) were purchased on January 2, last tax year, for $10,000 each, a total of $20,000. The Section 179 deduction was not taken on the trucks 3 and 4.

6. Other income and expense items relating to the business are as follows:

   a. Purchase of various small tools, $1,500
   b. Rent on office building, $8,400
   c. Gas, oil, insurance, and other truck expenses, $13,500
   d. Employee salaries, $104,000
   e. Office supplies, $1,200
   f. Taxes paid, $12,000
   g. Licenses and fees, $4,000
   h. Beginning inventory of materials was $4,500; purchases of materials amounted to $123,000; and ending inventory was $7,200.
   i. Legal and professional fees amounted to $2,500 of which $200 was for preparing the Holly's personal tax return.
   j. This year, Roger wants to use the Section 179 deductions to the extent he can.
   l. Revenues from the business amounted to $340,000.

7. Possible itemize deductions included the following:

   a. Real estate taxes, $600
   b. Personal property taxes on cars, $340
   c. Bank home mortgage interest, $8,700
   d. Interest on bank credit cards, $1,050
   e. Contributions to their church, $5,500
   f. Investment in an IRA account at the bank, $4,000: $2,000 in Roger's name and $2,000 in Barbara's name

REQUIRED: Complete the Holly's federal income tax return using TurboTax for Windows.

PROBLEM 15 Alan Myers

Objective: Foreign Moving Expenses, Foreign Earned Income, Itemized Deductions Decision making

Alan Myers, social security number 435-97-0423, is a petroleum engineer employed by Petro Consulting, Ltd., 654 Crescent Ave., Kuwait City, Kuwait. Petro Consulting's office in the United States is 7710 Alamo Lane, Dallas, Texas. Petro Consulting is a foreign entity. Alan's address in Kuwait is 11B Al Fahim Square, Al Ahmadi, Kuwait.

Alan is a single individual with no dependents. He moved to Kuwait on January 3. He remained there for most of the year, except for a brief trip back to the United States to visit his family, from July 1 to July 10. During the year, Alan was paid a salary of $75,500. In addition, he was given a home leave allowance of $3,000 so that he could visit his family in the United States. For the year, Alan had $6,500 of qualified housing expenses associated with his stay in Kuwait. Because there are no taxes in Kuwait, Alan wishes to take advantage of the foreign earned income exclusion. Assume that Alan's tax home is in Kuwait (he expects to remain employed by Petro Consulting in Kuwait for at least 2 more years.)

Additional information needed to complete Alan's tax return is provided below:

1. Alan owns some unimproved real estate in Seal Rock, Oregon. The real estate taxes on the property for the year were $1,080.

2. Alan gave two qualifying cash charitable contributions during the year -- $1,800 to University of Colorado, and $2,000 to Amnesty International, a US corporation qualifying under IRC 502(c)(3).

3. Alan paid $2,400 for medical insurance. In addition, he paid $200 for eyeglasses, $150 for dental checkups, and had $600 of other medical expenses -- none of these expenses were reimbursed by his insurance.

4. Alan paid $50 for a safe deposit box, $400 for tax preparation, $300 for professional dues and journals, and $500 for unreimbursed employee business expenses (for a firefighting suit made of Kevlar and asbestos.)

5. Alan incurred several expenses related to his move to Kuwait in January. Information related to the move is provided below:

   a. Cost of moving his personal effects and household goods was $6,000.
   b. Cost of travel to Kuwait: $875 airfare and $80 for meals.
   c. For the first 14 days that Alan was in Kuwait, he stayed at a hotel (costing $70 per night), while he searched for permanent housing. During his hotel stay, the cost of his meals was $392.
   d. Before moving to Kuwait, Alan was employed as a petroleum engineer in Houston, Texas.

6. Alan does not support the Presidential Election Campaign Fund. The only foreign financial accounts he has is his checking account at the Bank of Kuwait. The average balance in that account was $1,000. The highest balance was just after receiving his paycheck and was $3,200.

REQUIRED: Complete Alan's federal income tax return using TurboTax for Windows

PROBLEM 16 Terry Arnold

Objective: Gross Income transactions, Net Operating Loss

Terry Arnold, SSN 231-23-1231, is a single taxpayer. She began work as a self-employed graphics designer in June. Terry lives at Rt. 1 Box 421, Lawn, PA 17041.

The following tax related events occurred during the year:

1. Terry won a TV set in a raffle held to benefit the high school band. The TV set cost the band $350. The set had a list price of $585, but was recently on sale for $455.

2. Terry has 500 shares of Bankadoo stock. A $1 per share dividend was declared December 15, 1997, which was payable January 15, 1998.

3. On January 5, 1997, Terry cashed a check from the state lottery for $2,500, which had arrived in the mail at her residence during the last week of 1996. Terry was on vacation and did not find the check until she returned on January 2, 1997.

4. Terry paid $9,000 in mortgage interest during the year on her home. In addition, she paid $1,070 in property taxes on her house and made a charitable contribution of $875 to her church.

5. To help finance her new graphics design business, Terry sold 5,000 shares of ZenCo stock. She had purchased the stock on July 1, 1991 for $32,000. The sales price of the stock on the date of sale, April 5, 1997, was $30,000.

6. Terry had $80,000 of gross receipts from her new business, Terry's Graphics Design. She also had the following expenses:

    a. Advertising, $4,500
    b. Office Rent, $6,400
    c. Computer Rental, $3,000
    d. Business License, $500
    e. Utilities, $1,200
    f. Office Supplies, $500
    g. Accounting/Legal Fees, $300
    h. Wages paid to part-time help $1,000

7. Terry does not support the presidential election campaign fund nor does she have any foreign financial accounts.

8. Prior to June, Terry was a student at the University of Lawn. During the spring semester, she received a graduate assistantship that required her to be a full-time student and to work in the college 10 hours per week. She received $2,500. She paid tuition of $1,800 and purchased $300 in books. The balance was used for food.

REQUIRED: Complete Terry's federal income tax return using TurboTax for Windows.

PROBLEM 17 Stuart Dent

Objective: Gross Income transactions, Final return

During the year, Stuart Dent, SSN 229-22-9229, was enrolled as a full-time student at Texas Tech. His school address was 467 Nashville Road, Lubbock, TX 79409. Stu also worked part-time at the University Book Shoppe (employer number 12-6767676). He earned $2,242 with $139 withheld for Social security and $33, for Medicare taxes.

During breaks and summers, Stu worked as a waiter at Mom's Home Cookin'. During the summer, he earned $800 in wages and $560 in tips. Social security taxes withheld amounted to $84 and Medicare taxes were $20. No federal income tax was withheld.

Stu received a $2,000 scholarship to help defray the costs of college. Stu's college expenses for the year included the following:

Tuition	$1,500
Books	$425
Food	$2,500
Lodging	$1,800

Stu paid $500 in estimated quarterly federal income tax payments, $125 at each payment date.

Several years ago, Stu received an inheritance from his grandmother consisting of several financial securities. Income from these investments are as follows:

1. Interest on State of Texas Bonds: $2,300
2. Interest on US Treasury bonds: $4,050
3. Dividend income:

    a. General Motors, $436
    b. IBM, $642
    c. AT&T announced a 2 for 1 stock split for date of record of July 10. Stu held 400 shares valued at $40 per share. His adjusted basis in the stock was $10,000.
    d. Apple Corp. distributed a 2% stock dividend, on September 15. This resulted in Stu receiving an extra 14 shares of stock when the value of the stock was $23 per share.

4. On December 28, Stu was on his way to Dallas to attend the Cotton Bowl. Stu was in a traffic accident, he fell asleep at the wheel. Unfortunately, Stu was dead on arrival at the Dallas hospital. The car was valued at $12,000 just before the accident. Stu's car was totally destroyed. The car insurance proceeds of $10,000, were assigned to the bank to settle the outstanding loan on the car of $8,000.

5. On December 29, Stu's paycheck for working at Mom's Home Cookin' came in the mail. The gross amount of the check was $300 with federal income taxes of $50, Social security taxes of $23 and Medicare taxes of $4 withheld. Stu's father cashed the check and used the proceeds for funeral expenses.

6. On December 30, Stu's father was going through some of Stu's things when he found a coupon bond registered in Stu's name. Father clipped the attached coupon and took it to the bank. The bank credited father's account for $135, the interest for the six months ending December 1.

Due to his financial independence, Stu's parents do not claim him as a dependent. Stu supported the political process and the presidential campaign fund. Stu will take the standard deduction.

REQUIRED: Complete the Stu's federal income tax return using TurboTax for Windows. You may need to perform some tax research to complete Stu's return.

PROBLEM 18 John Fauchon

Objective: Small business transactions and estimated tax

John Fauchon is a self-employed painter. His social security number is 261-16-1261 and his address is 231 Main St., Chicago, IL 60666, and his telephone is 312-555-5544. John is single and operates Fauchon Painting out of his rented home. He uses the second bedroom as his office. The bedroom is 500 square feet. His home has a total area of 2,000 square feet. John's rent for his house is $250 per month ($3,000 per year) and his total utility costs for the year were $1,600.

John grossed $142,000 in his business during the year. He operates under the cash method of accounting and has essentially no inventory at year end. The costs of materials and outside labor amounted to $44,000. In addition he incurred the following expenses:

1. Advertising costs were $1,200
2. Insurance costs were $2,300
3. Legal and accounting costs were $500
4. A customer refuses to pay a $4,000 bill. John talked to his attorney and determined that taking the case to court would not be cost effective, so he is giving up on collecting the bill.
5. John leases all of his equipment. His leasing costs for the year amounted to $5,700.
6. John paid $3,600 during the year for his health insurance coverage. Fortunately, he was healthy the entire year and did not incur any medical expenses.
7. His telephone bill for the year was $1,200 which included business related long distance calls of $400. The monthly charge for phone service was $60 per month. He estimate that 75% of his local calls were business calls.
8. In addition to his home telephone, John purchased a cellular phone which he carries with him in his rented truck. The phone cost $150 and the phone charges for the year were $240. John estimates that 30 per cent of the calls on this phone are personal; 70%, business related.

John's income varies greatly. His taxable income last year was only $35,000. He had paid no estimated taxes for that year, thus in April of the current tax year, he paid $4,900 in federal income tax, $4,945 in self-employment taxes, and $1,800 in state income taxes when he filed his tax returns. On December 15, 1997, he paid $10,000 in estimated federal taxes. This was his only payment of the year. John does not want to contribute to the President Election Campaign Fund.

REQUIRED: Complete John's federal income tax return using TurboTax for Windows.

PROBLEM 19 George and Barbara Foley

Objectives: Property transactions and potential hobby loss

George and Barbara Foley are married with two children, Sam 4, and Ted 12. Social Security numbers are, respectively: 212-12-1212, 121-21-2121, 234-34-5345, and 222-33-4444. They live at 706 Caroline Street, Frederick, MD 21701. Child care for Sam was provided by Frederick's Playland, 80 South Street, Frederick, MD 21702, employer ID number 12-5675432, and cost $5,200 for the year. Ted was old enough to take care of himself, but not old enough to take care of Sam.

George works for the investment banking firm, Churnum & Burnum, employer number 12-23412334. His salary was $47,000 and withholdings were as follows: Social security, $2,914; Medicare taxes, $682; Federal income, $7,620; and state income, $1,200. George also made federal estimated tax payments of $1,000 per quarter as scheduled.

George's salary, in addition to investment income, allows Barbara to pursue her love of painting. This endeavor is not yet profitable, but Barbara reasons that most great artists are not recognized in their own time. She spent $1,200 on supplies and other expenses and sold 2 paintings for $400 each. Her federal tax ID number is 23-3456789.

The Foleys financial activities during the year include:

1. They sold 400 shares of IBM on July 5, for $46 per share. 200 shares were purchased eight years ago on May 4, for $50 per share. Three years ago the stock made a 2 for 1 split, when the value of the stock was $60 per share.

2. During the year, the Foleys moved across town, a total of 52 miles. Churum & Burnum wanted their employees to live in the best part of town. Their former home was 31 miles from George's place of employment, and their current home is 20 miles from George's work. George paid the moving company $1,500 for the move. His employer gave George a moving grant of $1,000 which was **not** reported on his W-2.

3. George and Barbara sold their former house for $80,000. The house had an adjusted basis of $60,000. They purchased their current residence for $100,000 two months after selling the old one. Both houses qualify as principal residences.

4. On July 5, the Foleys sold 200 shares of APCO stock for $5,000. The original cost of the stock was $3,000 when it was purchased exactly three years earlier. Also on July 5, they purchased 100 shares of Consolidated Edison stock, also for $5,000. Both stocks are utility companies with equivalent risks and returns.

5. On October 12, Barbara paid Arthur & Price, CPAs, $1,500 for preparing a cash projection and business plan for an art gallery to be located in Frederick. Barbara decided not to go into the business at this time, but perhaps later. A&P advised her that now was not the best time to start a new business.

6. George is concerned about the high cost of college tuition (so is everyone else.) Accordingly he invested $1,000 in the Growth Mutual Fund in Sam's name and $3,000 in Ted's name to the same fund. George retained the right to sell the shares for the boys' benefit. The Growth Fund reported dividends of $30 and long-term capital gains of $100 to Sam; dividends of $90 and long-term capital gain of $300 to Ted. This is the only income received by Sam and Ted during the year.

7. George and Barbara do not support the presidential election campaign fund.

REQUIRED: Complete the Foley federal income tax return using TurboTax for Windows.

PROBLEM 20 Carol Gatti

Objective: Small Business Return

Carol Gatti, social security number 612-21-4567, rents a house at 613 Indiantown Road, Hasty, CO 81044. Carol's telephone number is 719-555-7654. She is single and operates a sole proprietorship selling computer equipment. Carol incurred the following transactions relating to her business and other tax-related activities during the year:

1. Office equipment costing $12,000, purchased in November and a delivery van costing $10,000 was purchased on June 1. She decided to elect Section 179 treatment.

2. Because she feels image is very important in this business, she bought a BMW 325i for $33,000 on September 1. It was used 90% for business.

3. Last year on January 1, $2,000 of office furniture was purchased. She did not elect Section 179 with regard to this asset.

4. Revenues from the business totaled $200,000.

5. Other information relating to their business is listed below:

    a. Advertising , $3,000
    b. Delivery van expenses, $2,000; BMW operating expenses, $4,000
    c. Accounting, $1,500
    d. Supplies, $800
    e. Utilities, $1,800
    f. Beginning inventory, $35,000; Purchases, $125,000; and ending inventory, $40,000
    g. Store rent, $16,000

6. Carol contributed $3,500 to a retirement plan organized under the Keogh plan provisions. The money was deposited on September 2.

7. Carol paid estimated federal income taxes of $30,000; estimated state income tax of $4,000. All of these taxes were paid during the current tax year.

8. Carol supports the Presidential Campaign Fund.

REQUIRED: Complete Carol Gatti's federal income tax return using TurboTax for Windows.

PROBLEM 21 Anthony Singlterry

Objectives: Investments and alimony

Anthony Singlterry, social security number 231-47-9748, is currently single with no dependents. He lives at 34 Hernrico Lane, Reading MA, 01867. His telephone number is 508-555-8765. Anthony works at United Parcel Service as a driver and makes $44,656 a year. Social security tax withheld was $2,769; Medicare tax, $646; Federal income taxes, $5,434, and state income tax, $1,409.

Ten years ago, Tony divorced his wife. The divorce agreement provided that he would pay alimony of $12,000 per year. In the current year, he paid his ex-wife $6,000 in cash and gave her stock in Apex Machine Corporation that was worth $6,000 on August 15, the day he transferred it to her. The stock had cost him $2,000 when he purchased it in August, 1989. She sold the stock on November 12, for $4,000. Tony's ex-wife's SSN is 521-86-9534.

Three years ago, Tony bought five $1000 Exxon corporate bonds at their face value. Due to the recent decline in interest rates the bonds are now selling at 108. Tony thinks that interest rates will climb in the near future, so he sold the bonds on July 8 for their current price, 108. Tony received $450 interest from the bonds during the year.

Tony also purchased some stock in a military defense startup company, HiTech Avionics, in late December, 1996, for $5,000. Unfortunately, the contract for a new missile guidance system that the firm was banking on was canceled due to cuts in the defense budget. The announcement came just 11 days later, on January 5, 1997. By the next day the stock was deemed totally worthless. He still held the stock at the end of the year.

Other stock transactions for the year included:

1. Stock in CAM Computer Corporation purchased on June 8, 1989 for $1,200 was sold on May 9 of this year for $5,000.

2. Stock in Lare BioTech which was purchased on November 7, 1996 for $5,400 was sold, at a loss, on May 7, 1997, for $1,500.

Tony supports the Presidential Campaign Fund and has no interest in any foreign accounts.

REQUIRED: Complete Tony's federal income tax return using TurboTax for Windows.

PROBLEM 22 Lewis and Vivian Willis

Objectives: Itemized deductions with casualty loss, charitable contributions

Lewis Willis (age 60) and his wife Vivian (60) live at 593 Depot Street, Indianapolis, IN 46291. Their social security numbers are, respectively, 423-54-7545 and 123-65-9345. They support the Presidential Elections Campaign Fund and may be reached at 317-555-5555.

Lewis works for the city of Indianapolis as a property assessor, and his wife works for BMG CD club as an order processor. Lewis and Vivian's W-2 information is as follows:

	Lewis	Vivian
Wages	$26,215	$21,642
Social security	$ 1,625	$ 1,342
Medicare taxes	$ 380	$ 314
Federal income tax	$ 2,252	$ 1,923
State income tax	$ 1,143	$ 947

Lewis and Vivian also paid property taxes of $1,400, mortgage interest of $627, credit card interest of $411. Their tax return preparation fee was $200. They also had considerable medical expenses as follows: insurance premiums of $3,500, prescription medication of $470, nonprescription medication $200, vitamins $150, and they also paid deductibles to doctors and hospitals in the amount of $1,500.

During the year, while the Willises were at the hospital, their house was robbed of the following possessions:

1. In March, Jewelry costing $3,000, which had a fair market value of $4,000, was taken. The insurance company reimbursed them the full market value of $4,000.

2. In August, other items that were not insured, with a cost of $3,000, and a fair market value of $2,000, were stolen.

The property was never recovered, but the criminals were caught. The Willises were so impressed with the way the police handled the incident that they decided to donate $1,000 to the Silver Shield Foundation, a qualified charity that supports the widows and orphans of officers that are killed in the line of duty.

The BMG CD club established a program five years ago that allowed its employees to purchase excess inventory items, CDs, at a discounted price. Vivian took advantage of the opportunity to purchase 500 CDs at a price of $2 each two years ago. The CDs had a regular price of $12.50 each. Vivian donated the CDs to the Indiana Home for Teens in Evansville, a qualified charity on September 3 this year.

Lewis has to use his personal automobile in his job because the city does not have cars for use by the assessor's department. The city reimbursed Lewis at a rate of $.20 per mile. Lewis submitted expense reports for 10,000 miles of traveling and received $2,000. In addition to these business miles, Lewis drove 20,000 personal miles during the year, of which 3,000 miles were for commuting. While he was away from the office, he incurred $500 in food costs for lunches. None of the lunches were reimbursed by the city.

For several years, Lewis has worked with the youth group at his church. During the current year, Lewis used his personal automobile to take the youth group on outings. He drove a total of 4,000 miles. The church did not reimburse him for the trips.

In early December, Lewis and Vivian traveled to Dallas to attend a national church meeting as a representative of their church. They spent a total of six days in Dallas. Five of those days they were in all day meetings. On the sixth day, they went to Six Flags. The total cost of the trip was $1,400. The church did not reimburse them.

REQUIRED: Complete the Willis federal income tax return using TurboTax for Windows.

PROBLEM 23 Christine Willard

Objectives: Contribution of property, vacation home, business loss

Christine Willard (age 40) is a widow whose husband died last year. She has two children Tommy and Susan ages 14 and 17. Christine has an unlisted telephone number. They all reside at 345 Lakeshore Drive, Florence KY 41022. The family's social security numbers are:

	SSN
Christine	435-41-5743
Thomas	376-43-1634
Susan	357-27-4536

Christine is a scientist at a local pharmaceutical firm. Her salary was $78,354 with the following amounts withheld from her salary:

Social security	$3,887
Medicare tax	$ 991
Federal	$9,876
State	$2,987

On May 3, Christine contributed stock in Computerland with a basis of $500 and a fair market value of $2,500 to Queen's Medical Research Fund, 111 Kailua, Honolulu, HI, a qualifying charity. The stock was purchased on June 14, 1986. Christine also had interest income of $6,000 from investments in corporate bonds.

Christine incurred $5,500 mortgage interest on her home, $975 real estate taxes, and interest on credit cards of $345.

Christine owns a condo on the beach at Myrtle Beach, SC. She used the condo five weeks this year for family vacations and trips. She rents the condo to other families the remainder of the year. During the current year, she rented the condo for a total of 10 weeks at $650 per week. The condo cost $100,000 when she purchased it after her husband died last year. (She used some of his life insurance money.) She paid the real estate firm $1,300 for managing the property. Since the condo was new last year, there were no repairs. Insurance on the property cost $1,200.

Additionally, Christine is working on developing a drug on her own that could help in the treatment of sickle cell anemia. In developing this drug, she incurred research and development costs of $60,000 this year and $50,000 last year. In response to positive publications, the Sickle Cell Anemia Foundation awarded her a grant of $3,000 to help in her research. Christine is hopeful of receiving a major grant of $2.1 million next year. Christine's federal employer ID number is 45-6789012.

Christine does not support the Presidential Election Campaign Fund.

REQUIRED: Complete Christine's federal income tax return using TurboTax for Windows.

PROBLEM 24 Douglas Clayton

Objectives: Employee Expenses, moving expenses

During the year, Douglas Clayton SSN 223-65-9686 and single, moved from Atlanta, Georgia, to 1504 Towne Ct., East Peru, ME 04229 in order to keep his position in his company, Big Biz, Inc., employer ID number 55-1234567. The company did not pay any of the costs of moving. His old home is 1,500 miles from his new job location and 30 miles from his old place of work. Doug incurred the following expenses in the move:

1. Moving personal belongings, $2,200
2. Travel to new residence, $1,400
3. Apartment hunting trips, $1,800

Doug's W-2 reports his salary as $45,750; social security tax, $2,836; Medicare taxes, $663; Federal income taxes, $10,850; and Maine income taxes, $2,400.

Doug Clayton is an account executive for BigBiz, Inc., a major industrial supplier. His job requires him to travel on occasion, but his employer does not reimburse him. The employer feels that his salary is sufficient to offset the expenses of his travel. Doug has adequate records for all of the items listed below:

1. Doug personally paid for two business trips during the year. The first trip to Des Moines, Iowa was spent entirely on business. Airfare cost $600, lodging cost $500, and meals and entertainment expenses were $325 for the one week stay.

2. The second trip was for five days in Las Vegas, Nevada. He arrived on Sunday evening and started with his business meetings on Monday morning. On Wednesday, he completed the negotiations and felt good about the week's work so far. The primary purpose of the trip was for business, but Doug finished business matters on Wednesday, and spent the last two days gambling. Hotel, meals and entertainment expenses were the same for each of the five days. The cost were Airfare, $625; lodging, $765; and meals and entertainment, $425.

3. Doug did reasonably well at the gaming tables in Vegas. The first day of gambling, he won $5,000. The second day he was not so lucky; he ended the day losing $3,000. Thus, he ended the trip with $2,000 profit from gambling.

Additionally, Doug drove his personal automobile 1,500 business miles. These miles were for trips around Maine on company business. On one occasion, he was late and drove a bit fast to make up the time. He got a speeding ticket that ended up costing him $250. His total miles driven were 25,000 including 2,500 commuting miles.

Doug's only other tax related transaction was his annual contribution to his alma mater, Georgia Tech. He gave $300 this year. He supports the Presidential Election Campaign Fund.

REQUIRED: Complete Doug's federal income tax return using TurboTax for Windows.

PROBLEM 25 Dennis and Pat Garnett

Objectives: Passive activities

Dennis and Pat Garnett live at 32 Wilshire Drive, Home, KS 66438. Their telephone number is 913-555-5645. Pat is a real estate assessor for New Realty Company, and makes $35,000 per year. Social security withholding was $2,170; Medicare taxes, $508; federal income tax, $3,342; and state income taxes, $1,000. Dennis stayed home to take care of their son, Johnny and look after the family's investments. Social security numbers are as follows: Dennis 213-54-7468, Pat 324-63-7143, and Johnny 132-77-6143.

Dennis materially participates in a rental real estate activity, The One (ID number, 11-2233445), which reported a loss of $15,000 for this year (they have sufficient basis to absorb the loss). Dennis was a limited partner in another real estate venture, called The Second (ID number 22-3344556), with a beginning of the year basis of $20,000 and a net loss of $25,000 for the year. Yet another of Dennis's limited partnership involving real estate, (you guessed it) The Third (ID number 98-7654321) generated a $10,000 gain.

During the year, the Garnetts agreed to an out-of-court settlement from which they received $20,000 in compensatory damages and $60,000 in punitive damages. The defendant was Billy Joe Bob Dupree, a local televangelist who made slanderous remarks about the Garnetts on his television program after the Garnett's partnership, The Third, refused to sell him some land near a lot Dupree already owned. It seems that without Garnett's lot Dupree will be unable to fulfill his dream of building the world's largest amusement park cathedral.

Other tax related transactions included the following:

1. Mortgage interest on their home was $4,600.
2. Mortgage interest on their mountain cabin was $3,900.
3. Medical bills paid in excess of insurance was $2,300.
4. Personal property taxes amounted to $235.
5. Real estate taxes amounted to $895.
6. Charitable contributions to his church $600.
7. Contribution of $1,000 to the Bobby Carter Fund, a fund set up at a local bank to help pay the expenses of a young man who broke his back while on his senior class beach trip. The family can not afford the $50,000 medical bill. There is no relation between the Garnetts and the Carters.
8. To call attention to the need for green plants, Dennis dug up a small cottonwood tree from his back yard and planted it on the courthouse lawn. The tree had a value of $100. The tree was on his lot at the time he purchased the property. He estimates that the value of the tree at the time he purchased his house in 1990 was $10.
9. They fully support the Presidential Election Campaign Fund.

REQUIRED: Complete the Garnetts federal income tax return using TurboTax for Windows.

PROBLEM 26 Mike and Mary Older

Objective: Retired executive with investment income

Mike and Mary Older are a retired couple who live at 4982 Burruss Road, Tempe, Arizona 85287. Mike is retired from his position as Chief Financial Officer for Bombay Furniture Company. Mike's social security number is 389-76-5421; Mary's, 367-43-9764, and their telephone number is 602-555-6786. After discussing their financial affairs for some time, you have gathered the following information.

1. Mike receives a yearly pension from Bombay of $45,000. The pension is a lifetime annuity on his life only which was funded entirely by his employer. Both Federal income taxes, of $12,000, and state income taxes, of $2,300, were withheld from the pension during the year.

2. The Olders have invested in the Growth Mutual Fund for several years. In the current year, they received ordinary income distributions of $63,000 and capital gain distributions of $28,000 from the fund. No federal or state taxes were withheld.

3. Other items of income received during the year included:

    1. Mike's Social Security receipts were $23,600.
    2. Interest Income received were as follows:

        a. Bank of Arizona, $3,200 on checking account
        b. Tempe Savings Bank, $4,450
        c. The Olders have no other accounts, foreign or domestic.

4. The Olders sold stock that Mike had received from Bombay under a non-qualified stock option plan. The stock was worth $250,000 at the time he received it in May, 1989. Mike sold the stock on December 4, 1997 for $342,000. He deposited the proceeds in his checking account while he considered what to do with the funds.

5. Mike has always been a supporter of education. In the July, a friend asked Mike to teach a class at Arizona State in Controllership. He agreed to do so. The university paid him $5,300 for teaching the class. It also withheld Federal income taxes of $480, social security taxes of $329, Medicare taxes of $77, and Arizona income taxes of $318. The faculty were pleased with Mike's performance and has asked him to teach again next semester.

6. Routine uninsured medical expenses included:

    a. Doctors, $800
    b. Prescription medicines, $400
    c. Over-the-counter medications, $350

7. Other expenditures made during the year include:

   a. Gift to their son, $10,000
   b. Cash contribution to Arizona State, $4,500
   c. Tax return preparation fee, $600

REQUIRED:

1. Use TurboTax for Windows to prepare and print the Olders' Federal income tax return. They fully support the Presidential Election Campaign Fund.

2. Advise the Olders' about what to do with the proceeds from the sale of their stock. For your information, State of Arizona bonds have an interest rate of 4%; average corporate bond rate is 8%; bank account rates are 5%; and the high risk bond rate is 12%.

3. Determine the marginal taxes on the income from teaching if Mike agrees to do so in the Spring. For this part, assume that Mike will invest the funds from Bombay in the bank and earn 5% on the funds for the year. Is this a wise strategy?

For these required items, consider simply modifying the data input and compute the new tax amount.

Problem 27 Bob and Sue Brown

Objective: S corporation earnings and potential AMT problems; Tax planning for AMT

Bob Brown is the owner of Brown Inc. a small manufacturing in Statesboro, Georgia that makes magnetic plastic strips that can be imprinted with businesses names and given to customers for their refrigerators. The business has been moderately successful the past few years. Since Bob considers his business to be a small business, he elected to be treated as a Small Business Corporation under Subchapter S of the IRC; hence Brown Inc is a S Corporation.

Bob and Sue live at 789 Fortin Ave, Statesboro, GA 30460-8141 and their telephone number is 912-555-7655. Bob's SSN is 443-76-1234 and Sue's is 454-78-8621. Brown Inc. taxpayer ID number is 77-9873621 and corporate headquarters are at 89 Martin Road in Statesboro; ZIP code 34060. Sue works at home caring for their two children Karen (age 10, SSN 245-76-8421) and Spence (age 7, SSN 265-66-3456,) and overseeing their home with its two acre garden named "Tara".

Bob's accountant prepared the Form 1120S and reported the following items on Bob's form K-1:

Line 1, Ordinary income (loss) from trade or business	($60,000)
Line 4a, Interest income	12,000
Line 4e, Long-term capital gain	50,000
Line 5, Net gain under Section 1231	18,000
Line 14a, Depreciation adjustment on property, after 1986	30,000
Line 14b, Adjusted gain or loss	8,000

In addition to the income and expenses from Brown Inc, Bob and Sue report the following items:

1. Sue purchased private activity bonds issued by the city of Statesboro in 1994. The interest from these bonds amounted to $10,000 for the current year.

2. Bob inherited a one-third interest in the family farm located outside of Florence, AL. The farm is operated as Brown Farms, Ltd., a limited partnership with Bob's brother Jim as the general partner and Bob and his sister Alma as limited partners. Bob's share of the farming profits this year is $20,000. According to the partnership agreement all expenses are allocated to the general partner, thus, there were no other items reported on the K-1 from Brown Farms, Ltd. Brown Farms, Ltd. tax ID is 55-3423126.

3. Bob received dividends of $26,000 from his portfolio of stock. He did not sale any of his stock during the year.

4. In 1996, Bob greatly overpaid his state income tax. His itemized deductions in 1996 amounted to $12,980; his 1996 federal tax was $13,000. As a result of the overpayment, Bob and Sue received a refund from the State of Georgia in 1997 of $5,000.

5. Bob and Sue's itemized deductions include the following:

a.	Local property tax on Tara	$4,300
b.	Georgia estimated income tax paid in 1997	9,000
c.	Mortgage interest, on loan used to purchase Tara	24,000
d.	Home Equity loan used to purchase auto	7,000
e.	Contribution to Georgia Southern University	8,000

REQUIRED:

1. Use TurboTax for Windows to prepare and print the Brown's Federal income tax return. They support the Presidential Campaign Fund.

2. Assume that the Brown's are considering some potential transactions that will be completed during 1997. Consider the impact on their federal income taxes of the following transactions. In other words, recompute the Brown's tax return assuming the following changes.

   a. Pay an additional $1,000 in estimated state income tax during the year.
   b. Make a charitable contribution of stock that has a basis of $5,000 and a FMV of $15,000. The stock would be contributed to Georgia Southern, their favorite charity.
   c. Sell some stock they own that would result in a $4,000 gain.
   d. Bob would like to know if there would be any advantage to him to have the corporation, Brown, Inc, elect the deduction under Section 179 on the $10,000 of qualifying equipment purchased during the year. The qualifying equipment is a personal computer, printer, and other computer equipment that he purchased on April 1. If the corporation elected Section 179, the corporation loss would increase by $6,500; depreciation for regular income tax would decrease by $3,500; AMT depreciation would decrease by $2,000; and Section 179 deduction would increase by $10,000 and would be reported on Line 8, of Bob's K-1 from the corporation.

   Modify Bob's tax return to account for these changes and print Form 1040.

PROBLEM 28 **Pat and Wilma Oceanview**

Objective: Comprehensive individual tax return

Pat and Wilma Oceanview live at 34 Ocean Street in picturesque Charleston, South Carolina, zip code 29409, and phone 803-555-6655. Pat is the controller for Nations Paper Corporation, which is headquartered in Charleston. Wilma (SSN 422-76-7392) owns and operates an advertising company that specializes in chemical and paper companies. They have two children -- Jon, SSN 233-87-5642, age 10; and Nancy, SSN 244-77-5643, age 15.

Pat's (SSN 443-87-9876) ~~salary for 1996 is $100,000~~. He contributes to a flexible benefit plan through a salary reduction agreement under IRC 125 in the amount of $6,500 per year, thus his W-2 shows gross salary of $93,500. In addition, the W-2 reports federal withholding taxes of $23,800 for income tax; $3,887 for social security taxes; 1,356 for Medicare tax; and $3,400 for state income tax.

Pat also reports that he traveled substantially on company business. In total, Pat spent $12,400 on airfare, $6,500 on lodging, $4,000 on food, and $500 on incidentals. Pat also used his personal car for 7,000 miles of business travel (commuting travel was 3,000 miles and personal travel amounted to 12,000.) Pat elects to take the mileage allowance for his allowable business miles. Nations Paper gives Pat a travel allowance of $30,000 to cover all his travel expenses. Pat then must account to the IRS for his expenses. Pat has all appropriate documentation for the expenses listed above. Pat's company makes a contribution to a qualified pension plan for his benefit in the amount of $10,000 per year. Also, the company provides basic medical insurance for he and his family. Additional health insurance coverage is available at a cost of $2,000 per year which Pat decided to purchase as a part of the flexible benefit plan. The other expenses paid by that plan, $4,500, are for part-time child care services.

Because of Pat's travel he received frequent travel miles which allowed him to get four roundtrip tickets that have a value of $2,200. He used the tickets to take the family on vacation.

Wilma has been very successful with her advertising agency. She uses the cash basis of accounting for tax purposes, operates as a sole proprietor, and reports the following information:

1.	Revenue	440,000
2.	Wages and benefits paid	103,000
3.	Office rent and expenses	45,000
4.	Professional services	120,000
5.	Magazine expenses	8,000

In addition, Wilma purchased specialized computer equipment that cost $65,000 on January 5. She wants to maximize her depreciation deductions and elects to maximize her Section 179 deduction.

Because of her interest in the print media, Wilma is investigating starting a monthly magazine that will address the problems of the chemical industry. She spent $8,000 doing a feasibility survey and investigating publication facilities. As of the end of the year, she is still uncertain if the time is right. Maybe next year. Her bookkeeper recorded the expenses as magazine expenses, item 5 above.

Pat paid federal estimated taxes of $35,000 and state estimated income taxes of $3,000 during the year. Other investment transactions are listed below:

1. Pat received interest from the Metro Life Insurance Company of $3,500. This interest is from a life insurance policy he owned on his first wife Helda who died 15 years ago. Pat elected to leave the policy proceeds with the company.

2. Pat invested in a limited partnership that owns and leases pulp wood hauling trucks to paper companies throughout the southeast. This year, the partnership reports Pat's share of the loss as $55,000. The partnership is named Trucks or Us and has a tax ID number of 44-8623457. It is located in Charlotte, NC.

3. Wilma is an one-third partner in Charleston Land Company which develops apartment houses. Her K-1 reports her share of the partnership's loss as $15,000. The partnership's ID number is 67-8527358. She meets monthly with here partners to review the month's business and to plan future projects. The meetings last about 4 hours each month.

4. Pat owns 450 shares of the Tax Exempt Mutual Fund (ID number 44-9988776) that invests only in bonds issues by states and subdivisions thereof where the interest is entirely exempt from federal income taxes. The fund reported that each share received $10 of interest income, long-term loss on sale of bonds of $2 per share, and long-term gain on sale of bonds of $1 per share.

Pat and Wilma reported the following itemized deductions.

1. Local property taxes paid of $1,200
2. Contributions to The Citadel, a state university in Charleston, $3,000
3. Tax preparation fee of $600
4. Interest expense on home mortgage of $12,000
5. Investment advice from Churum and Burnum Investors, $300
6. Tax advice from Arthur & Price, CPAs $800

In addition, Pat and Wilma had a fire on October 1, at their beachfront condo. The fire completely destroyed the condo and its contents. The condo had cost $75,000 12 years ago and was valued at $130,000 at the time of the fire. The contents had cost $23,000 and were valued at $15,000 at the time of the fire. Their insurance paid $120,000 for the condo and $12,000 for the contents. They accepted the payment with regret. The related land was valued at $200,000 before the fire; it increased to $210,000 after the fire.

To make things worst, Pat was his fishing boat shortly after the fire when he turn the throttle the wrong way and crashed into the pier. The boat had cost $13,000 and was valued at $8,500 was completely destroyed. He did not have any insurance. Fortunately, Pat only suffered a server headache from the lecture Wilma gave him about the lack of insurance.

Prior to the fire, Pat and Wilma had rented their condo to summer vacationers. During the year prior to October 1, they had rented the condo for 13 weeks (91 days). In addition, they had used the condo for 30 days; the remainder of the time, the condo was not used. The mortgage interest on the condo amount to $4,000; property taxes were $800; repairs amounted to $500; insurance was $1,000; fees paid to rental agent was $1,000; and revenue from rental fees was $10,400.

They told you that they fully support the Presidential Election Campaign Fund and that they have no interest in foreign bank accounts.

REQUIRED: Prepare the Oceanview's federal income tax return.

All expenses must be prorated/allocated

PROBLEM 29 Bob and Sally Mickels

Objective: The purpose of this problem is to provide a comprehensive tax return problem that may be work in parts. Each part after the first may be added or deleted as your instructor wishes.

It was a story book marriage. Bob and Sally Mickels were married on a riverboat traveling down the Mississippi, on New Year's Eve, December 31, 1996. The weather was picture perfect as they said their vows. Since gambling is legal on the boat, and it was Bob and Sally's day, they tried their hand at roulette. Before the night of gambling was over, Bob had won $12,000 and Sally had won $21,000. They started gambling at 8 PM and stopped at 1 AM on January 1, 1997, when the honeymoon began. The riverboat recorded their winnings and gave them checks for their winnings less 20% withholding. Bob's check was for $9,600 (withholding for federal income tax was $2,400); Sally's check was for $16,800 (withholding for federal income tax was $4,200). What a wedding day indeed!

Bob and Sally live at 456 Easy Street, Memphis, TN 38150, telephone 901-555-6766.

Bob (SSN 432-43-2534) works as a weatherman for WBTV in Memphis, Tennessee. For the year, the station paid him a salary of $58,000 from which it withheld $14,400 for federal income tax; $3,596 in social security tax; and $841 in medicare tax. The station's federal ID number is 66-8573623 and address of record is 6677 Beale Street, Memphis, Tennessee 38152.

Sally (SSN 234-87-6523) Mickels is an advertising executive for Blue Moon Ads, Inc. in Memphis, Tennessee. In 1996, she received a base salary of $55,000 from which Blue Moon withheld $13,200 for federal income tax; $3,410 in social security tax; and $797.50 in medicare tax. Blue Moon's federal ID number is 68-4528536 and address of record is 5600 Beale Street, Memphis, Tennessee 38152. In addition, Sally received a bonus check for $14,000 on Friday, December 30, at 4:55 p.m. Sally and Bob had left town to attend the Sugar Bowl in New Orleans, and did not return to Memphis until Monday morning, January 2, 1998. Sally found the check and took it to the bank at noon on Monday. No taxes were withheld from the check.

Part A: Prepare a joint tax return for Bob and Sally Mickels assuming that they use the standard deduction. Both Bob and Sally fully supports the Presidential Election Campaign Fund.

Part B. The story of Bob and Sally continues.

On February 1, Bob formed the Bob Mickels Production Company, a sole proprietorship engaged in the production of television and radio commercials. As a new company, Bob Mickels Production Company has had a rough time getting established. Bob made a strong effort during February, March and April to meet all the right people. During that three month period, he had lunch with potential clients on fifty different occasions. Bob paid for all these lunches, a total cost of $1,000 of which Bob estimated his meals cost half, $500. From this effort, Bob gain three clients. Time for Plan B.

During the rest of the year, Bob hit the golf club. He joined the Memphis Country Club (initiation fee $2,500; monthly club fees of $50, a total of $400 paid during the year) and played golf frequently. He did not play well -- a source of embarrassment to him and his potential clients. So he took golfing lessons from the club pro at a cost of $500. It helped, he played better, made a better impression and got new clients for his production company. Bob incurred $600 in food purchases directly related to his business, and $400 in personal charges. In addition, on December 28, Bob paid the first six months of monthly dues for 1998, a total of $300.

For the eleven months of 1997, Bob Mickels Production Company billed clients for $120,000 in fees. However, as of December 31, Bob had only collected $56,000. When he returned to Memphis after the Sugar Bowl trip, he found checks for $15,000 in his Monday mail. The envelopes containing the checks were postmarked on December 31. In addition to the promotion expenses above, the company had wages expense of $15,000 for a secretary; rent on studio and office space of $33,000; payments to independent contractors for camera operators, video engineers, and others technical support people of $45,000; and rental of equipment of $25,000. The independent contractors work for various television stations in the Memphis area and did the work for Bob on a part-time basis.

Neither Bob's nor Sally's employer provides health insurance for its employees. To provide some protection, Bob joined the Farm Bureau (membership fee $10) and purchased health insurance from Blue Cross and Blue Shield that covered both Bob and Sally. He paid $300 per month for this health insurance.

To help pay the bills from the production company, Bob borrowed $80,000 from the National Bank of Memphis and paid $6,600 in interest.

Part B. Prepare Bob and Sally's joint tax return considering the information in Part A and Part B.

Part C. And yet there is more about Bob and Sally.

In late February, Sally and Bob signed up for a seminar on a cruise boat focused on basic accounting and reporting for business. The seminar covers topics on both recording and using accounting information. The brochures says that the seminar is "designed for both business owners and managers of businesses." The cost of the seminar was $300 per person (both Bob and Sally paid); the cost of the cruise and related air fare was $1,800 per person, double occupancy. The cruise ship sailed from Miami, traveled around the Caribbean stopping at Puerto Rico and the U.S. Virgin Islands, and returned to Miami.

In March, Bob and Sally purchased their new home on Easy Street. They paid $22,000 as a down payment; assumed an outstanding mortgage of $70,000 with an interest rate of 8% on which they paid $4,300 in interest. To complete the purchase of the loan, they took out a personal loan (not a mortgage on the house) at the National Bank of Memphis for $30,000 with an interest rate of 7% on which they paid $1,600 in interest. They hope to pay the loan off next year and did not want to incur the costs related to obtaining a mortgage.

Other itemized expenses they incurred are as follows:

a. Cash contributions to their church, $2,000
b. Cash contribution to University of Memphis, $3,000
c. Sales taxes on new car, $350
d. Property taxes on their house, $800
e. Contribution to the Memphis Shelter Home of used furniture that cost $3,500 and had a FMV of $800 according to the Memphis Appraisal Company. Bob paid this company $35 for the appraisal. The shelter home is a 501(c)(3) corporation.

All was not rosy for Bob and Sally during the year. In November, Sally was caught in a sudden ice storm in Memphis (rare indeed) while driving home. As a result of the ice, Sally wrecked her car. The cost of the car had been $25,000. Its estimated value before the wreck was $16,000; its estimated value after the wreck, $10,000. The insurance settled the case and paid $3,000. Sally sold the car "as is" to a dealer for $9,500. She replaced the car with a car costing $19,500.

Part C. Prepare Bob and Sally's joint tax return considering the information in Parts A-C.

PROBLEM 30 Jim and Charlotte Lamewood

Objective: Home office, AMT problems, Passive Losses and Contributions

Jim and Charlotte are dedicated school teachers who have been the backbone of the Monroe County, West Virginia school system for several years. The live in Possum Hollow on Route 4, Box 433, Bluefield, West Virginia 26506, and their telephone number is 304-555-6774. Over the years they have been able to invest in a variety of projects including coal mines, real estate ventures, and even the stock market.

Jim's SSN is 589-23-8641 and he is head librarian at Bluefield High School. His salary is $34,000 with federal income tax withholdings of $4,800; social security tax of $2,108; medicare tax of $493; and state income tax of $1,350. The school system also contributes to a qualified retirement system and provides full health insurance coverage.

Charlotte's SSN is 836-16-2648 and she teaches fifth grade at the Westside Middle School. Her salary is $33,000 with federal income tax withholding of $4,500; social security of $2,046; medicare tax of $479; and state income tax of $1,245. The school system also contributes to a qualified retirement system and provides full health insurance coverage.

Nearly 17 years ago, Jim inherited some money from his father which he invested in the Blue Hill Mining Partnership. Jim is the limited partner with a 40% share of profit and losses. Ben Blue is the general partner. Jim's basis in Blue Hill Mining at year-end was $10,000 and the partnership has no liabilities. Jim's K-1 reported the following:

Line 1, Ordinary income (loss) from trade or business activities	$12,000
Line 15d Depletion (other than oil and gas)	62,000

Jim and Charlotte jointly own four real estate investments. They are listed below:

1. 250 acres of mountain land which they hope to sell to a ski lodge development that has been discussed for several years. The property taxes on the land are $2,500; mortgage interest on the outstanding mortgage on the land is $3,700; and they paid $50 for additional liability insurance on their home owners policy relating to land. In addition, Jim spent four days walking over the land looking it over and doing a little hunting while he was there. He spent $80 on gas on these trips.

2. A four unit apartment building at 453 Hill Street, Bluefield. The apartments are rented. For the year, the total rent was $14,400. The apartment building was purchased in five years ago for $86,000. Mortgage interest amounted to $4,000 for the year. Property taxes were $3,400; utilities paid by the Lamewoods amounted to $500; repairs were $450; and insurance costs $750.

3. A small rental house at 34 Mountain Lane, Bluefield. The house is rented for $3,000 a year. The house was purchased 12 years ago for $24,000. Mortgage interest was $800; property taxes were $400; utilities paid by the Lamewoods amounted to $200; repairs were $650; and insurance costs $150.

4. A community shopping center at 1000 Mountainview Drive. The center has two large stores and eight smaller stores. They purchased the center on January 2 of the current tax year for $950,000. The contract allocated $150,000 to the land, $70,000 to the parking area improvements, $10,000 for the center's office equipment, and $720,000 for the buildings. The rental income for the year was $154,000. Expenses included repairs to the roof of $22,000; property taxes of $31,000; insurance of $4,000; utilities of $6,000; and interest on the mortgage of $76,000. The parking lot was in bad shape and had to be repaved during the year. The cost of repaving the lot was $25,000 and was done on May 3. The paving company suggested paving the lot every ten years. Jim also employs his sister Marylou to manage the center. He paid her $22,000 including benefits. Marylou is a very competent manager, thus Jim and Charlotte only spent four hours in December reviewing the year with Marylou.

Jim and Charlotte's stock transactions for the year were limited. They believe in the investment philosophy of buy low and hold long. Actually they had only two transactions. On April 4, they sold 2,000 shares of GEE for $45 per share. They had purchased the stock on August 5, 1988, for $40,000. They paid sales commission of $8,000. On December 3, they donated 1,000 shares of BDE stock to West Virginia University, their alma mater. The stock was listed on the New York Stock Exchange at $87 per share on that date. They had purchased the stock on July 8, 1983 for $17 per share.

Dividend income from their portfolio is $6,300.

Other transactions include:

a. Home mortgage interest of $4,000
b. Cash gift to their church $2,500
c. Annual Cash gift to WVU, $1,000
d. Property taxes on their home, $300
e. Supplies purchased for use in teaching at school, $430

Jim and Charlotte have taken one bedroom and converted it to an office. The room is 15% of their total square footage of their home. They paid $65,000 for their home when purchased. Their utilities amounted to $1,500 per year; monthly telephone charges are $24 per month ($288 per year) and they estimated 40% of the calls relate to either school or their real estate investments; offices supplies cost $250 of which half related to school and half to their investments; and insurance on their home cost $300. Recall that the property taxes and mortgage interest are listed above.

Jim and Charlotte support the Presidential Election Campaign Fund and have no interest in any foreign accounts.

REQUIRED: Prepare Jim and Charlotte's federal income tax return.

INDEX

Register now to receive information about program and tax law updates.

Be informed of program or tax law changes!

Register your copy of TurboTax® today and you'll automatically be informed of program updates or last minute tax law changes that may occur.

Free Technical Support!

Register today and you'll receive access to our dedicated TurboTax technical support services—with expanded service, 7 days a week, January 12th–April 15th.

Free TurboTax Newsletter!

When you register, you'll receive the TurboTax Advantage newsletter, filled with helpful tax tips...and special offers on popular software products!

Register today!

To register your copy of TurboTax, fill out and mail the attached postage-paid registration card, or take advantage of our on-line registration after you install TurboTax.

Detach here and mail

TurboTax CD-ROM Final Registration

☐ **Yes!** Register my copy. Please add my name to your list of TurboTax users so I can receive information on program updates and last-minute tax law changes.

Name ______________________ (First) ___ (MI)

______________________ (Last)

Address ______________________

City ______________ State ____ Zip ________

Daytime Phone (___) ___-____ (Area Code)

E-Mail Address ______________________

Do you file a Schedule C? ☐ Yes ☐ No
(Profit or Loss from Business)

SC 561283 1445

IMPORTANT!
Register **NOW** to Receive
Information on
Program Changes

NO POSTAGE
NECESSARY
IF MAILED
IN THE
UNITED STATES

BUSINESS REPLY MAIL
FIRST-CLASS MAIL PERMIT NO. 1040 SAN DIEGO, CA

POSTAGE WILL BE PAID BY ADDRESSEE

Intuit
PO BOX 28857
TUCSON AZ 85775-2699

STOP!
Register Your Product.

So we can keep you informed
of program updates!

Read prior to installation
TurboTax License Agreement

Do not use the Software (which term includes the product documentation) until you have carefully read this Agreement, which provides the terms and conditions for its use. Installing the Software indicates that you have read, understand and accept this Agreement. If you do not accept this Agreement and purchased the Software from a retail store, then return the Software and accompanying items to that store within 30 days of purchase with a dated receipt for a full refund. If you purchased the Software directly from Intuit, contact Intuit and return it with the same information to Intuit Returns, 6060 Nancy Ridge Drive, Suite 100, San Diego, CA 92121-3290.

Permitted Uses and Restrictions on Use. You are granted a personal, non-exclusive license to use one copy of the Software and any final edition thereof only on a single computer and a single terminal. You may make one archival or backup copy of the Software for your own use. However, because the Software is protected by the copyright laws, it is illegal: to make additional copies or otherwise duplicate the Software by any other means (including electronic transmission); to give copies to another person; or, to modify, adapt, translate, rent, sublicense, loan, resell for profit, distribute, create derivative works based upon or network the Software or any part thereof. The Software also contains Intuit trade secrets, and you may not decompile or otherwise reverse engineer the Software.

You may not use the Software to prepare tax returns, schedules or worksheets on a professional basis (i.e., for a preparer's or other fee for tax preparation services). Notwithstanding anything in this Agreement, Intuit has no responsibility or liability for damages or claims relating to any use of the Software or the Services on a professional basis.

Electronic Filing Services. If you choose to file your return electronically, your tax return will transmitted by modem via the Internet to Intuit's Electronic Filing Center, where it will be converted to a standardized format and, then, transmitted to the applicable federal or state taxing authority (the "Services") while Intuit retains any records required by law. Intuit cannot guarantee that the taxing authority will accept your return due to circumstances beyond Intuit's control (e.g., incorrect user information, malfunction of the tax authority's system, etc.). Additionally, the telecommunications delivery systems used for Intuit's electronic filing services, such as the Internet, can be unpredictable in their performance and may, for example, impede access to Intuit's electronic filing service or the performance of the Services from time to time. You agree that Intuit is not in any way responsible for any such interference with your use of or access to the Services. Further, Intuit may at any time change or discontinue any aspect or feature of the Services including, but not limited to, its availability.

Satisfaction Guaranteed. If you are not 100% satisfied with this Software, Intuit's entire liability and your exclusive remedy shall be to remove the Software from your computer and return it within 90 days of purchase to the store where you purchased it with a dated receipt for a full refund. If the store is unable to issue a refund, or you purchased the Software directly from Intuit, then return the Software within such 90 day period to Intuit Returns, 6060 Nancy Ridge Drive, Suite 100, San Diego, CA 92121-3290.

Limited Warranty. If the disks are defective, then return the Software to Intuit Returns, 6060 Nancy Ridge Drive, Suite 100, San Diego, CA 92121-3290 within 60 days of purchase with a dated receipt, and replacement disks will be mailed to you.

Intuit warrants to its registered users the accuracy of the calculations on every form prepared using the final version of the Software (i.e., not any planning version). If you pay an IRS or state penalty and/or interest solely because of a calculation error on a form prepared using the final version of the Software and not as a result of, among other things, your failure to enter all required information accurately, your willful or fraudulent omission or inclusion of information on your tax return, your misclassification of information on your tax return, or your failure to file an amended return to avoid or reduce your penalty/interest after Intuit announced updates or corrections to the Software in time for you to file an amended return, then Intuit will pay to you the amount of the IRS or state penalty and/or interest paid by you to the IRS or state. In order for Intuit to notify you of updates or corrections to the Software, you must register the Software. If you believe such a calculation error occurred, please notify Intuit in writing at

Office of the President, Intuit Inc., 2650 East Elvira Road, Suite 100, Tucson, AZ 85706-7180 as soon as you learn of the mistake (and in no event later than 30 days after the penalty is assessed). You must include a copy of the IRS/state notice, a copy of the applicable hardcopy tax return and a diskette with the applicable tax return data file on it. Of course, you are responsible for paying any additional tax liability you may owe and providing any other information Intuit reasonably requests.

DISCLAIMER OF WARRANTIES

Except as expressly provided above, this Software and the Services are provided "as-is" and, to the maximum extent permitted by applicable law, Intuit and its suppliers disclaim all other warranties, express or implied, regarding the Software or Services, disk and related materials, including their fitness for a particular purpose, their quality, their merchantability, or their noninfringement. Intuit does not warrant that the Software or Services are free from bugs, interruption, errors, or other program limitations. Some states do not allow the exclusion of implied warranties, so the above exclusions may not apply to you. In that event, any implied warranties are limited in duration to 60 days from the date of purchase of the Software. However, some states do not allow limitations on how long an implied warranty lasts, so the above limitation may not apply to you. This warranty gives you specific legal rights, and you may have other rights which vary from state to state.

Tax laws and regulations change frequently and their application can vary widely based upon the specific facts and circumstances involved. Users are encouraged to consult with their own professional tax advisors concerning their specific tax circumstances. Intuit disclaims any responsibility for the accuracy or adequacy of any positions taken by users in their tax returns.

All warranties or guarantees given or made by Intuit with respect to the Software or Services (1) are for the benefit of the original purchaser/licensee of the Software only and are not transferable, and (2) shall be null and void if a purchaser/licensee breaches any terms or conditions of this Agreement.

LIMITATION OF LIABILITY AND DAMAGES

Except to the extent of the above warranty of calculation accuracy, the entire liability of Intuit and its representatives for any reason shall be limited to the amount paid by the customer for the Software or Services, as applicable, purchased from Intuit or its authorized reseller. To the maximum extent permitted by applicable law, Intuit and its licensors, distributors, dealers or suppliers are not liable for any indirect, special, incidental, or consequential damages (including damages for loss of business, loss of profits or investment, or the like), whether based on breach of contract, breach of warranty, tort (including negligence), product liability or otherwise, even if Intuit or its representatives have been advised of the possibility of such damages and even if a remedy set forth herein is found to have failed of its essential purpose. Some states do not allow the limitation and/or exclusion of liability for incidental or consequential damages, so the above limitation or exclusion may not apply to you.

The limitations of damages or liability set forth in this Agreement are fundamental elements of the basis of the bargain between Intuit and you. You acknowledge and agree that Intuit would not be able to provide this product on an economic basis without such limitations.

Miscellaneous. This Agreement sets forth Intuit's and its representatives' entire liability and your exclusive remedy with respect to the Software and Services, and is a complete statement of the agreement between you and Intuit. Headings are included for convenience only, and shall not be considered in interpreting this Agreement. This Agreement does not limit any rights that Intuit may have under trade secret, copyright, patent or other laws. The agents, employees, distributors, and dealers of Intuit are not authorized to make modifications to this Agreement, or to make any additional representations, commitments, or warranties binding on Intuit. If any provision of this Agreement is invalid or unenforceable under applicable law, then it shall be, to that extent, deemed omitted and the remaining provisions will continue in full force and effect. The validity and performance of this Agreement shall be governed by California law (without reference to choice of law principles), and applicable federal law. This Agreement is deemed entered into at San Diego, California, and shall be construed as to its fair meaning and not strictly for or against either party.

Export Restrictions. You acknowledge and agree that the Software is subject to restrictions and controls imposed by the International Traffic in Arms Regulations and Arms Export Control Act (the "Acts"). You agree and certify that the Software will not be shipped, transferred or exported, directly or indirectly, outside the United States or Canada, nor will it be used for any purpose prohibited by the Acts; provided, however, US citizens and US permanent resident aliens may travel to countries not prohibited by the Acts with the Software when it is installed on their personal computer and not otherwise used or transferred in violation of the Acts.

U.S. Government Restricted Rights. This section applies to any acquisition of the Software by or for any unit or agency of the United States Government (the "Government"). The Software shall be classified as "commercial computer software", as that term is defined in the applicable provisions of the Federal Acquisition Regulation (the "FAR") and supplements thereto, including the Department of Defense (DoD) FAR Supplement (the "DFARS"). Licensor represents that the Software was developed entirely at private expense, that no part of the Software was first produced in the performance of a Government contract, and that no part of the Software is in the public domain.

If the Software is supplied for use by DoD, the Software is delivered subject to the terms of this license agreement and either (i) in accordance with DFARS 227.7202-1(a) and 227.7202-3(a), or (ii) with restricted rights in accordance with DFARS 252.227-7013(c)(1)(ii) (OCT 1988), as applicable.

If the Software is supplied for use by a Federal agency other than DoD, the Software is restricted computer software delivered subject to the terms of this license agreement and (i) FAR 12.212(a); (ii) FAR 52.227-19; or (iii) FAR 52.227-14(ALT III), as applicable.

If the Software is delivered to a distributor, reseller, integrator or other non-Governmental entity (the "Intermediary") for ultimate delivery to the Government, either directly or through other intermediaries: (1) the Intermediary shall obtain no rights in the Software except the right to deliver the Software to the Government under the terms provided herein; and (2) the Intermediary shall not alter or remove any proprietary rights legends placed on the Software by Licensor.

First printing October 1997.

Want your TurboTax Software on 3.5" floppy disks instead of CD-ROM?

We'll send them directly to you $4.95

Thank you for puchasing TurboTax®!
If you'd like to have your TurboTax software
on 3.5" floppy disks instead of CD-ROM,
use one of these 3 easy ways to order:

1. Complete the order form below and return it to
Intuit Personal Tax Group
P.O. Box 28857
Tucson, AZ 85726-8557

2. Call Intuit at 1-800-624-9066

3. Fax the order form to Intuit at 1-800-756-1040

Priority code: 561283

Limit one product per order form. Only original order forms will be accepted.
Please fill in using dark blue or black ink only.

Complete this form, detach it and mail to :

Intuit Personal Tax Group, P. O. Box 28857 Tuscon, AZ 85726-8557

Name ______________________ _____
First MI
____
Last
Address______________________________
City ______________________________
State __________ Zip ______________

Choose **ONE:**
☐ **TurboTax (**Windows 3.1) on 3.5" floppy disks
☐ **TurboTax (**Windows 95) on 3.5" floppy disks

Software Cost $4.95

Sales Tax _____
Please add all applicable state and local sales/use taxes based on the destination of the order. All shipping and handling subject to tax except in AK, CA, IL and NJ.
Intuit reserves the right to correct all tax rates and/or collect all sales and/or use tax required by law.

TOTAL _____

Payment Method
Charge my ☐ VISA ☐ Mastercard ☐ Discover ☐ AMEX
Card # ☐☐☐☐☐☐☐☐☐☐☐☐☐☐☐☐ Exp. Date ☐☐/☐☐
☐ I prefer to pay now by check for the full amount (payable to "Intuit")

Signature ______________________________